Morag Robertson Aug '90

Listening
to the
Inner Self

Selected Books Written by Lucy Freeman

FIGHT AGAINST FEARS
THE STORY OF ANNA O
FAREWELL TO FEAR
WHO IS SYLVIA?
FREUD REDISCOVERED
WHY PEOPLE ACT THAT WAY
FREUD AND WOMEN
HOPE FOR THE TROUBLED
THE CRY FOR LOVE
THE STORY OF PSYCHOANALYSIS

Listening to the Inner Self

LUCY FREEMAN

Jason Aronson, Inc.
New York and London

Library of Congress Cataloging in Publication Data

Freeman, Lucy.
 Listening to the inner self.

 Bibliography: p. 201
  1. Psychotherapist and patient. 2. Psychoanalysis.
3. Langs, Robert J. I. Title.
RC480.8.F7 1983   616.89′17   83-9988
ISBN 0-87668-640-4

CONTENTS

ACKNOWLEDGMENTS

For the idea of this book and for his encouragement all along the way, my thanks to Dr. Jason Aronson. For her sensitive and expert editing, and for her support, I thank Joan Langs. And deepest thanks to Dr. Robert Langs who gave generously of his time and of his thoughts. I cannot omit Melinda Wirkus and Angie Miloszewski for their expertise in editorial production and design.

1
PRELUDE TO
A QUEST

Sometimes one does a book for the fun of it.
Or to learn.
Or for love.
Or revenge.
Or the wish to help others.
Or money.
Or to compete.
Or for reasons unknown.
And sometimes for several or all of these reasons.

D r. Robert Langs was to be a speaker at the 1979 midwinter meeting of the American Psychoanalytic Association in New York and my curiosity as a writer about psychoanalysis was aroused.

Langs' book, *The Bipersonal Field*, I had read with much interest. He considered the analytic experience an interaction between patient and analyst rather than patient and analyst existing in separate worlds—the patient speaking and the analyst interpreting.

The analytic meeting was held traditionally at the Waldorf Astoria, in midtown Manhattan. In a special room off the ballroom, publishers displayed their latest psychoanalytic works. I wandered in and saw Dr. Jason Aronson—publisher and psychoanalyst. He had published Langs' fifteen books.

As I leafed through the latest Langs, I said to Jason, "His theories intrigue me though I don't quite understand them."

"Why don't you listen to him?" Jason asked. "He's speaking here in twenty minutes."

I sighed. "I don't go to speeches, if I can help it, Jason. After thirteen years of covering all sorts of meetings for *The New York Times,* I promised myself when I left I would never listen to another speech. Now I read learned articles and books in the quiet of my room, or interview analysts in hotel corridors at conventions."

"You would enjoy Bob," Jason said. "He never makes a speech. He conducts a dialogue with the therapist who presents a case."

It is still difficult for me, even after many years of analysis, to say no to a man in authority (shades of my lawyer father) though I am doing far better these days. I was interested in learning more about Langs however so I followed Jason into the expansive Empire Room, to the left of the Park Avenue entrance of the Waldorf.

Two men were seated on the dais, Langs and a psychiatrist

from Los Angeles. Langs introduced the psychiatrist, who proceeded to describe a patient's first session. Langs then explained the way he listened to patients and how this patient was unconsciously conveying reactions to the psychiatrist's breaking important ground rules of therapy—starting the session ten minutes late, sharing an office with a colleague, employing a secretary. The two words "ground rules" are the cornerstone of Langs' work, they thread through his theories. Along with one other word, "deviation." A deviation from a ground rule in some subtle way harms the patient.

The deviations, Langs was saying, were connected to a new way of listening to the patient. A way involving an unconscious communication that somehow differed from the traditional unconscious communications analysts thought patients made. As a patient, I had never been aware of communicating anything, consciously or unconsciously, to the analyst. Let him figure out what I am saying and what he wants to say, if he wants to say anything, I had thought many a time as I lay in fury, silent, at his silence.

After the meeting, as I walked the few blocks home in the bitter cold, cursing the analysts for always picking the iciest week in the year to convene in New York, I thought about how Langs conveyed his theories in public. He had listened carefully as he heard, for the first time, the psychiatrist's case, then commented with conviction and spontaneity on the technique. This was different from reading Langs; his voice was persuasive, there was a sense of drama in the interplay between the two therapists.

Psychoanalysis offers a unique relationship. A relationship that exists no other place and at no other time in life. The therapist is the only one to whom we dare expose painful feelings and conflicts as we seek his expert help in easing unhappiness. To stop what Freud called "internal bleeding." The therapist can help ease the pain or push us further into the miasma of mental misery.

From Freud on, analysts have been aware that the emotional interaction between patient and analyst is as important as the intellectual. But little has been written about this in the analytic literature. Langs is the first to dedicate a body of work to what Freud called "countertransference," Langs' *leitmotif*. Freud defined countertransference as all the analyst's feelings, including hostile and erotic, aroused by the patient. "Transference" encompassed the patient's feelings for the analyst, which reflected the patient's transfer of childhood emotions toward his mother and father and traumatic experiences with them.

Langs looks on the relationship between patient and therapist as "interactional." He maintains it has been the practice of analysts to believe that the words of patients relate only to past traumas. But, he says, in addition, what the patient chooses to speak of about the past does not come out of the blue but is stimulated by and connected to the highly interactional relationship between patient and therapist. The therapist's every word and act spurs the opening or closing of the gates to the traumatic past. It is the therapist who stimulates each image and each fantasy that comes to the patient's mind, whether it centers on a recent experience or forms a memory from childhood.

"What the patient recalls about his past does not arise in a vacuum," Langs says. "The past usually comes up in relation to something the analyst has triggered. The patient as a rule does not go back for the sake of going back."

Langs emphasizes the *interaction* between patient and therapist and how it affects treatment. He also looks critically at the technique of psychoanalysts and all others who indulge in therapy of a different quality, as they become involved in the tenuous, delicate and complex task of helping people feel better.

By highlighting this sensitive issue, Langs has flung the psychic gauntlet not only to the ignorant, the corrupt, the shoddy, the faddist therapists but also to a number of classical analysts. His perceptive eye focuses sharply on all types of patient–therapist relationships, whether the patient lies on the couch or sits in the chair. Langs maintains that his responsibility is to the patient who is suffering because of ineffective treatment, analytic or otherwise.

Freud advised the analyst to act as a "mirror," not to express feelings or in any way interfere with the patient's thoughts by personal intrusion. Later analysts modified this image of the analyst, pointing out Freud did not mean it literally. After all, how could any human, even one supposed, unrealistically, to have solved all his conflicts, possess no ambivalent feelings of love and hate for the patient on the couch? A patient who, though tormented, was apt to be contentious, provocative, complaining, self-pitying, self-denigrating, self-absorbed, seductive and angry.

The image of the analyst as wholly objective and under complete control of his emotions was unfair to the analyst in that he was expected to deny all feelings (and analysts know well the psychic penalty imposed for this iron defense). The therapist may at times resist becoming aware of unpleasurable feelings; no one is ever fully analyzed for that is, like being perfect, an illusion. The self-analysis analysts are expected, per Freud's advice, to conduct all their lives following a personal analysis or analyses (many have had two or three) is a difficult task. And it is one thing for an analyst to be aware of his feelings, another to decide whether to express them. There may be times he wishes to show sympathy, for instance, if the patient is suffering a temporary illness. The essential question is how to be human without being intrusive. A robot-like therapist is apt to frighten the patient, hardly to instill trust.

It is vital to effective therapy to reconstruct and understand the past, but this is only part of the psychoanalytic process, according to Langs. He lists three curative factors and says no one of them will cure if the other two are missing:

1. Insight — the understanding of the traumas of the past.
2. An identification with the therapist that is positive and strengthening and leads to a sense of trust, which gives the patient the courage to face the repressed feelings and fantasies he has believed dangerous to his self-esteem.
3. The providing by the therapist of a psychological "holding" or "containing" that gives the patient a sense of emotional security as he begins to become aware of threatening feelings within. This holding, Langs believes, emanates from the therapist's ability to adhere to the ground rules Freud devised.

Langs charges that therapists, including some psychoanalysts, break a number of the ground rules that define the analytic relationship. The rules govern the locale of treatment, the confidentiality due the patient, the fee. Langs calls these boundaries and their

creation by the therapist "the core conditions of treatment." He believes that when the therapist breaks one of Freud's ground rules
(plus a few added since his death), a patient will keep complaining
about the psychic injury suffered as a result of such deviation. It
takes precedence over all the psychic injuries remembered since birth.
Since the analyst has now become the most important person in the
patient's life, as was the mother of infancy, whatever the analyst
does to hurt or reject comes first.

Langs arrived at these conclusions by listening to patients in
what he calls "a new way." In terms of their conscious and unconscious fantasies as related to the interaction with the therapist. Langs
realized, he says, patients were sending unconscious messages related to something the therapist said or did or failed to do. And that
this had set off a chain of unconscious interaction, provoking the
patient to deliver as protest special unconscious messages.

Not unexpectedly, Langs has become controversial in psychoanalytic and other therapeutic circles. Some call him a heretic and
a renegade. But in spite of strong opposition he is supported by a
growing number of psychoanalysts, psychiatrists, psychologists and
social workers who believe he is contributing new effectiveness to
psychoanalytic technique. His adherents make peace with his seemingly merciless focus on the therapist and his errors. In addition to
private practice in New York, he lectures nationally and abroad in
Sweden, Italy and Great Britain.

He has become, as Jason Aronson described him, a spokes-
person for the patient, the Ralph Nader of psychotherapy. Langs
is asking not only analysts but all therapists to give more effective
treatment by observing the boundaries that make the patient feel
emotionally safe enough to trust the therapist.

Langs is asking therapists to be more aware of the unconscious
meanings of their words and acts so they will not unknowingly inflict the hostile and sexual feelings unresolved in their own personal
analyses on the patient. Many analysts now treat patients for five,
ten, sometimes fifteen years. Psychoanalysis becomes longer as more
is discovered about the psychic processes of the early years of life
and their influence on later behavior. Most patients expect the analyst to be perfect but this is transferring onto the analyst their illu-

sion about their parents in childhood. However, patients should be able to expect an analyst to be aware of ways he might be hurting the patient, or at least to offer the best of help in terms of present practice.

I was writing *Freud and Women* with Herbert S. Strean, a psychoanalyst, president of the Society for Psychoanalytic Training established by Reuben Fine. As I researched this book, I became aware that Freud, genius though he was at theory, had difficulty in his treatment of some patients. A few contemporary psychoanalysts wrote articles about his hostility to an eighteen-year-old girl, Dora, one of his early cases at the turn of the century. Freud seemed to blame her for her emotional distress rather than trying to help her uncover her conflicts. He was described as never having faced his hatred of women, based on ambivalent feelings about his mother. But, I thought, this was when he first started to practice, and he certainly in his lifetime gave women enough by making it possible for them to achieve emotional freedom and emphasizing how important it was for them to possess it — I would hate to think of my life without Freud.

Seven months passed. One morning I received a phone call from Jason. After the pleasantries, he asked, "How about doing a book on Bob's work?"

"He's done fifteen," I said in surprise. "What more could I possibly add?"

"Those books are for the professionals," Jason said. "This would explain his work to the public."

"Why would the public want to know?"

Jason answered swiftly and pointedly, "So they can choose their therapists more wisely."

His words went straight to my heart. I have always crusaded for "let the buyer beware" in mental health. Freud had feared his discoveries would be "distorted and diluted" in America, a true prophet. The wild therapies that had sprung up like poisonous psychological weeds owed their existence to Freud. He proved we do not have to suffer emotionally, that if we can face our distorted fantasies we can control our lives more rationally. The trouble is, during what I think of as these pioneer days of standing one-half step out of the psychic jungle, it is difficult to find qualified therapists, and troubled people tend to rush to anyone who promises instant relief.

"How about it?" Jason was saying.

"I don't know if this is my kind of book."

I did not feel sure Langs was completely Freudian. My entire professional life, as well as personal one in analysis, was Freudian. To say one word against my savior would be swallowing hemlock, so to speak, destroying my faith in my hero and my work.

"Why don't you want to do it?" Jason's tone was warm and coaxing.

"I've always been a champion of classical analysis," I explained.

"So is Langs. He's more classical than the most classical analyst."

"You think so?"

"You've read his books."

I sighed. It seems I was always sighing around Jason, which meant I felt conflicted. "I wish I really understood what he was saying," I protested.

"I have an idea," Jason said. "Attend the seminar he is conducting for five days at his summer home in Long Island. There will be about ten students from all over the country. You'll pick up what Bob is saying."

It was late July, I had been working steadily for a year and wondering if I could get away for a week's vacation, leave *Freud and Women* behind.

"You can take your bathing suit," Jason was saying.

I could pick up seashells, bake on the beach, live on lobster.

"Can you arrange it?" I asked.

"Consider it done," he said. "You can stay at his house."

I could hear Langs explain his theories to the muted chorale of waves breaking on the long stretches of sand. The detective in me, long occupied in trying to solve the small murders committed daily in fantasy by the human mind (principally my own), as well as in writing about the motives of real murderers in books and articles, wanted to discover even more psychological clues (myriad in each life) to the origin and power of our sensual and murderous wishes.

I also wanted to find out what Langs was saying that so intrigued Jason that he had published fifteen of Langs' books. Books that sold very well all over the world.

I could do worse for a vacation, I thought, as I hauled out my bathing suit of green and blue, colors of the sea. I would also take along to reread on the three-hour train ride eastward toward the Atlantic, Langs' latest book, *The Psychotherapeutic Conspiracy*. I recalled a passage that had struck me with its eloquence. Something about the pain of the patient who seeks analysis. The pain suffered in the past and the new pain of exposing this agony at long last to a stranger in the hope of easing it.

I felt that passage propelling me toward Langs' Long Island beach.

2
SEMINAR OF A DIFFERENT KIND

The train rolled, lurched and rocked its way through the picture-book towns of Long Island. In the distance at Central Islip rose the fortress-like Pilgrim Psychiatric Center, which houses 3,000 of those so emotionally ill they need to be locked up so they will not harm themselves or others.

These tormented souls are described by the professionals as at one end of the spectrum of emotional disturbance, with the so-called "neurotic" in the middle and, at the other end, the relatively emotionally mature. Those who "knew themselves" and lived temperate, reasoned lives. There were some therapists who believed the "psychotics" capable of being helped through psychoanalytically based therapy, and were giving this help.

Recent figures from the United States Public Health Service showed there were roughly 6,700,000 men, women and children in this country in some form of therapy with 1,600,000 therapists. Of these, 2,700 are graduates of the twenty-six institutes accredited by the American Psychoanalytic Association that accept for the most part only applicants with medical degrees. No one knows how many have been trained in the tradition of Freud or Jung or Adler or Horney or other institutes or societies that accept the nonmedical person.

Because of Freud's essential philosophy that man did not have to endure a life of "quiet desperation," to quote Thoreau, if able to face the torment within, millions seek to relieve their mental agony. But there are not as yet nearly enough adequately trained therapists out there in the psychic wilderness. Many therapists manipulate, exploit, command, advise, accuse, seduce or otherwise waste the money of the desperate, sometimes making them more emotionally disturbed, sometimes causing suicides.

In *The Psychotherapeutic Conspiracy* Langs minces no words about the abysmal state of psychotherapy. It is peopled by "wild, mad therapists." He says even a number of the classical psychoanalysts fail to give effective treatment because they sacrifice "an essential piece of the truth." I had taken this bumpy ride because I wanted to find out what Langs meant by "essential piece."

It is not Freud's theories of psychoanalysis but the *technique* of psychoanalysis — how the therapist cures or fails to cure, or could cure more effectively — with which Langs is concerned. He believes that what takes place between patient and therapist is not in the patient's best interest if the therapist does not understand his crucial part in what goes on between patient and therapist. Not the intellectual action — the battlefront on which the conscious part of the mind engages. But the far more critical battleground where the emotional action takes place and where unconscious interplay may remain unperceived by therapist as well as patient, and serve as enemy to both.

According to Langs, as far as I understood him, therapists who do not try to be aware of their own sexual desires stirred by the patients, as well as feelings of dislike, irritation and even intense hatred, cannot help patients beyond what may be temporary easing of such symptoms as headaches, sinusitis, and ulcers. The therapists will fail to reach the deeper layers of the mind, both their own and the patients', where buried conflicts seethe.

I would see, I hoped, the way in which Langs was training therapists in what he called the "missing link" of technique. This focused on the therapist's ability to understand what the patient was conveying through messages that dealt with ground rules the therapist was breaking or interpretations that were meaningless or hurtful.

When I arrived at Langs' summer home, he welcomed me, fed me a sandwich, then showed me to a first-floor bedroom looking out on dunes. I unpacked with that peaceful sense of feeling soothed by the sound of ocean waves. I breathed in the fragrance of unpolluted air, wondered if there would be time to roam the near-by beach.

Then I heard voices on the sun deck outside my window, saw figures assembling for the seminar. I joined them, introduced myself. There were nine men and two women. They came from Texas, Oregon, Florida, Ohio and Johannesburg, South Africa, to take part in this experiment in supervision which was to start at 1 P.M. on August 8, 1982.

The traveler from Johannesburg, an amiable psychoanalytically oriented psychiatrist, Dr. George Warren, explained to me in a clipped British accent why he had taken the seventeen-hour flight: "After reading Langs' books I was fascinated with his theories. He seems to be talking a language I understand and want to know more about."

Of the four psychiatrists, one had trained at the Menninger School of Psychiatry in Topeka and one of the four psychologists had also trained there. One of the three social workers was a woman; the other woman was a psychiatrist.

Several members of the group had heard Langs lecture or had received supervision over the phone or learned his theories from tapes. One psychologist, Attilio Capponi, was on the faculty of the Psychotherapy Training Program of the Lenox Hill Hospital in Manhattan, which had been founded by Langs. Another psychologist was a student in the same program.

Langs greeted his guests and announced the five-day seminar would start with this four-hour session, breaking after two hours for a stretch. Then he settled his six feet, two inches into a chair as we circled him. We would be oblivious for the next hours to the dunes and dwarf firs surrounding us, the roar of the ocean three houses away.

Langs has a deep, mellifluous voice that conveys his intensity, and sometimes his impatience with the waste of a second. He has a rapid-fire way of speaking when he wants to make a point as his green eyes look steadily at you. In spite of sitting weekdays listening to patients or writing books and articles, he keeps slim by playing tennis on the island in summer and indoors in Manhattan in the winter.

Wanting to stimulate us at once, Langs started with a statement that revealed both his respect for Freud yet his questioning of Freud's technique. He said: "Freud's theories are still the primary basis of the entire psychotherapeutic field. But treatment of the patient, which is different from theory, or dynamics, is a treacherous area. No real guidelines have been developed. The papers on 'cure' are amorphous. While Freud gave us a relatively valid explanation of the instinctual drives and their vicissitudes — the nature of emotional disorders — his method of treating a patient was created mainly in the service of his own defenses. And the development of psychoanalysis, ever since its start, has been thwarted by the defensive needs of therapists who have clung steadfastly to Freud's way of treating patients. Their interpretations serve the need of the therapist, not the patient.

"After all, despite his self-analysis, Freud, as is true of all of us, had major defensive needs. An approach that stresses communication between patient and therapist shows that under most conditions our defensive needs take precedence over virtually all other needs. Freud was no exception.

"For example, he had great difficulty with the seduction hypothesis, a topic of recent controversy. At first he believed emotional disorders were founded on the actual childhood seduction of children by their parents or others close to the child. During Freud's self-analysis he theorized these reported seductions were figments of the imagination of his patients — fantasies rather than realities. He did so in spite of an indelible early memory of his own mother standing nude before him as she changed into her nightgown aboard a train going from Leipzig to Vienna, where the family moved when Freud was four-and-a-half.

"Freud fluctuated between an insistence that the seduction memories of patients were fantasies and acknowledgment that actual childhood seductions took place and influenced neuroses. While I could make many comments on Freud's defensive needs in this area, since our focus is to be on psychotherapeutic techniques, I will select an impression that is a bridge from his theory of psychology to his method of analysis. I would say that one of the reasons he had a defensive need to deny the reality of either subtle or blatant seductions of children by parents or others was that Freud himself was a highly seductive psychoanalyst. In denying the clinical seduction hypothesis, he was denying the seductive aspects of himself and his own technique with patients.

"As a result, Freud introduced the concept of transference — that the patient responds erroneously and pathologically to the analyst, based *entirely* on displacement from a past experience with his mother or father. Freud's concept of transference was a way of denying contribution to what his patients were experiencing and communicating to him. Freud's own defensive needs led him to mistaken formulations regarding the patient's communications in treatment. And, as a consequence, the very nature of psychoanalytic intervention."

Langs added quickly, "It is profoundly humbling to realize that in all likelihood, without these defenses available to Freud and his followers, the psychoanalytic movement would never have come into being. I thing Dr. Josef Breuer, Freud's colleague, could not invoke the concept of transference as a defense against his own probable realization that he had been seductive with his patient, Anna O. Confronted on some level with his own guilt, he simply fled the budding psychoanalytic movement.

"But Freud was able to deny his seductiveness. When one patient threw her arms around him after a session that probably included full body massage, hypnosis and a home visit — Freud's technique in those early days — he said her embrace had nothing to do with his personal charm and therefore he could propose the source lay elsewhere, that is, in a seductive relationship with her father.

"Armed with such denial as protection, Freud could remain a psychoanalyst to his death. In fact, the truths contained in what I call 'encoded communications from patients' are so perceptive of fallibilities in therapists that their recognition has been intolerable to both patients and therapists during the first one hundred years of psychotherapeutic practice."

He concluded: "Thus Freud gave us a creative heritage but he also gave us a defensive approach to treatment. Whatever the patient says is laid off on the past — the mother and father of childhood. Therapists insist they are innocent of provoking any reaction. As most of you know, it is the purpose of this seminar to help each of you recognize these truths about yourself when they are communicated by your patients. And to tolerate their instant analysis of you. This intensive course is designed to give you the technical means with which to cope with your patient's expressions without undue defense and anxiety. Such achievement, as you already know, is by no means a small accomplishment."

Langs then settled down to an explanation of the "communicative approach." He conducts the training of students by listening to one after another describe how he or she manages a therapeutic session. Langs then discusses this management in terms of whether the therapist has "heard" what the patient is saying. Langs' approach centers on the task facing therapists when they receive hidden messages from the patients' unconscious mind. These messages often refer to errors on the part of the therapists that have provoked fear or rage in the patients that is intense enough to halt any progress into explorations of past conflicts.

Langs said to us, "We'll loosen up by listening to a case and see if the patient's messages get decoded by the therapist. And then we'll see if the patient validates the therapist's interventions. My listening process requires such validation. We'll take into consideration the breaking of ground rules and the kind of interventions therapists make. In our listening we will be quite speculative and tentative. These are just practice exercises."

The female social worker asked, "Will you explain what you mean by validation?"

I blessed her for I did not have the vaguest idea and would not have asked, at this seminar I was the silent observer and note-taker.

"Every intervention by a therapist should obtain from the patient a clear validation," Langs replied. "The revelation by the patient of an encoded message that supports, enhances and gives fresh meaning to the area in which the therapist has intervened."

"And exactly what is an 'intervention'?" the social worker asked.

"Anything the therapist says or does or does not do that pertains to the management of the session," Langs said.

Then he asked, "Who's going to present the first case?"

The presentation was undertaken by James Winter (to protect the identity of therapist and patient, names have been changed, as well as the locale in which treatment was carried out). Winter is a young clinical psychologist whose office is in an outpatient psychiatric clinic. He volunteered to describe a first session with a patient.

This first session is always an extremely important one, accord-

ing to Langs and most analysts. At this time, the entire tone of the
therapy is set by the therapist. Patients are usually anxious and the
first impressions of a therapist are crucial to treatment; I well recalled
my first close encounter with a psychic world of a different kind.

Winter read from a report he had written, not in the presence
of the patient, for this would be breaking a ground rule, he explained,
but after the patient had left. Winter started off: "The patient was
referred to me by a psychiatrist who said the patient could not afford
his fee of eighty dollars. My fee is fifty dollars."

Langs commented, "Let's pause here. We begin, as therapy so
often does, with the breaking of a ground rule by the therapist. We
will see how such a break constitutes what I call the patient's 'adaptive
context'. We will then examine that adaptive context through decoding
what the patient says. We will then listen to the patient's validations
of our decoding. This is the hallmark of a communicative approach.
We let the patient's derivatives answer our questions. As the
derivatives always do when the patient faces something that causes
him anxiety."

A male social worker asked, "What ground rule has been
broken?"

"It's not a matter of a broken ground rule in this case but it
constitutes a cause of anxiety to a patient — being turned down by
one therapist and referred to another for a lesser fee. The patient
will have many images about the second therapist."

The social worker asked, "Such as that the second therapist isn't
as good as the first because he doesn't charge as much?"

"Yes. The patient will be somewhat traumatized by losing a
sense of security in being rejected by the first therapist. That will
be a heritage for the second therapist. In private practice there should
be mention only of a single fee."

Dr. Warren, the psychiatrist from South Africa asked, "Why
is it breaking a ground rule to take notes in the presence of the
patient?"

Langs answered, "To write about the patient in his presence is
to intrude on his privacy and disrupt his attention from his thoughts.
If you want to take notes, do it right after he leaves."

I thought of one of my analysts, a strict Freudian in her late sixties, who took occasional notes. One day I finally mustered up the courage to protest, asking, "Why do you take notes?" She said curtly, "Do you have to get all my attention — like a little child?" I felt rebuked, humiliated, and never said another word about the note-taking. Now I realized I had been justified in feeling angry and upset. Thank you, Dr. Langs, I said silently.

Langs was saying to Winter (as I took notes on a therapist, sweet revenge), "Please continue."

Winter went on: "The patient called and explained he was looking for help as a condition of his release from prison. The parole board had suggested he see a therapist because he had been convicted of a violent crime."

"This is far from the usual patient," Langs pointed out. "This man in a sense has been coerced into coming for treatment. But let's see how Winter handles him."

"He said he would be bringing insurance forms," Winter continued. "I set a time and gave directions to my office, which is hard to locate. I work in a clinic in a hospital." He added somewhat apologetically, "Next to the electroshock room."

We all laughed at the irony of this, knowing the effect on the patient. He would now fear not only the clinic situation, which hardly guaranteed privacy, but also the proximity to electroshock. The entire setting spelled danger.

Langs, who had joined in the laughter, said thoughtfully, "Our laughter signifies the patient's anxiety. We can start to identify some of the characteristics of our listening process by trying to understand the patient's adaptive context. First, he probably feels put down after being sent by the original therapist to the second. We will keep searching for other adaptive contexts. There can be none, or one, or several or many. Depending on the therapist."

The adaptive context seemed one of Langs' important concepts. It related somehow to the errors the therapist made, that much I knew. It was like pouring black ink into a glass of clear water. The adaptive context colored the free associations of the patient, which could no longer be thought of as "free" but focused on what the patient felt as injury or rejection.

Langs was saying to Winter, "Remember now, you've got two

major tasks. One, to identify your own interventions in terms of their implications, and two, to listen to the patient's material in terms of his picking up your interventions and then decode his unconscious message. You have to identify from his spoken words the theme or themes that relate to his underlying image of you — what I call the raw or threatening image."

Then he made the important point, "The patient will be afraid to tell you directly what he is thinking. He does not even consciously know it. He feels there is as much danger in becoming aware of what he perceives about you as in telling you directly. But if you listen, you can hear his valid perceptions of your errors through the images of you he communicates unconsciously."

A psychiatrist asked, "Could you give us an example of what these perceptions might be?"

"His perception of Winter may well be that he is 'inferior' to the first therapist," Langs said, "though we will need his words to confirm this. He also told Winter he would bring insurance forms and perhaps he is telling Winter he is insuring himself against 'cheap therapy', but we will also need his words to confirm this. We may hear from him words to the effect that 'You've got a deviation, you're taking me at a lower fee from a third party, the higher-priced therapist who turned me down, so I'll take my deviation in the insurance forms. You're not going to get me alone in the room with you, you're too dangerous'."

A psychologist asked, "Why is it a deviation to accept insurance?"

"Any third party observer or payment constitutes a deviation," Langs said. "A third party impairs the patient's sense of confidentiality. It compromises the treatment. The more you take part in deviating from the ground rule of not accepting any third party, the further away you push insight from the patient. I have never failed to see a patient who was accepting insurance who did not present a catalogue of destructive implications in his free associations. Insurance provides a form of pathological gratification — getting something for nothing, having a proxy mother by your side. You hear a lot of images about addiction from a patient when there is insurance. It's necessary at times for therapists to work under such a deviant condition but they should recognize that it is a compromise and try to do as much as they can either to eliminate it or minimize its effects as an adaptive context."

"Please explain what you mean by 'adaptive context'," a psychiatrist requested.

Hurrah, I thought, maybe now I'll understand it, and poised the pen carefully.

Langs explained, "The interventions of the therapist create the triggers, or the stimulus, for the patient's free associations. What I call the adaptive context *is* the trigger, *is* the stimulus or stimuli. In this case so far the triggers are the two different fees, the sending of the patient from one therapist to another, the insurance forms and the location of Winter's office in an unsafe place, as the patient would view it — little confidentiality in a clinic, and next to electroshock therapy."

He added, "The adaptive context includes the way a therapist creates a setting. The patient responds to all the errors and intrusions of the therapist in terms of his image of the therapist. A therapist who deviates is seen as dangerous, perverse, seductive and entrapping, all of which sets the patient off into flight.

"In this case, the patient's fear, anger and confusion, along with other complex reactions, will appear in disguise early in the session. A patient has two tasks — to tell the story of his life and symptoms, and to encode the story of his experience with the therapist up to this point. The patient's unconscious perceptions of the therapist always take precedence over his own problems. We are all defensive human beings and if someone gives us *his* problem, we work over it before we do our own because it is easier. It causes less conflicts than facing our own hidden dangers."

Aha, I thought, now I understand why so many of us are busy trying to solve the problems of other people rather than setting our own lives straight.

Langs warned Winter, "You must know what the patient's image of you is before you make an intervention. Please go on."

Winter continued calmly (I was admiring his patience, what with all the interruptions from Langs and the others, whom Langs encouraged to speak), "I set his first hour for 6 P.M. the next day.

Promptly at that time, my phone rings. The patient's voice says, 'Here's the security guard downstairs. Tell him where your office is. I can't find it'."

The group realized this was confirmation of the patient's concern about a third party, as well as indication of his fear of the setting. Coming into contact with a security guard would also remind him of his prison experience, hardly ease his already intense fear of "hospital" and "clinic" and "electroshock."

Langs said to Winter, "Reality is lending you a hand for unconscious communication, as it always does. Here your patient finds himself in a hospital clinic heading towards an electroshock room and appealing to a security guard to help him locate you. It's like bringing a protector."

A psychologist asked Langs, "Do you believe patients should not be treated in clinics?"

Langs answered this question thoughtfully. He said, "Because I emphasize keeping the ground rules and focus on the implications of all deviations, therapists sometimes get the mistaken impression that I'm saying treatment cannot be done under compromised conditions — which means in any place other than a private office with a separate entrance and exit so that patients do not see each other. But nothing is further from the truth. I believe there are two forms of treatment, 'secure frame' therapy and 'deviant frame' therapy. In the coming century it seems clear a lot of patients will be seen under deviant conditions in clinics, hospitals and shared offices, that is, shared with other therapists. My main goal is to try to get therapists to be aware of the impact these deviations will have on them and on their patients, and to listen to the patients' material with the deviations as the adaptive context. And to the material that follows from the patients as their encoded perceptions of the therapists in light of these deviations.

"We have to focus on these issues because the conditions of treatment constitute the heart of the therapeutic relationship. So, to answer your question, treatment can be done in a clinic but we have to look at the deviations as the adaptive context and as part of the interventions of the therapist to which the patient will respond. Because that's where all meaning will be, at first.

"If you recognize this, it is then possible to treat these patients, to help them understand the implications of being seen in a clinic, and to go on from there. If clinics realize these implications, they can eliminate many of the deviations. In this instance, by moving the office far from the electroshock room, or by having a separate entrance and exit for patients so they are guaranteed a sense of privacy."

A social worker said to Winter, "It seems to me your patient is mimicking his referral to you, sent from one therapist to another. Like he's telling you, 'You're a helpless fool who doesn't know where he's at, who allows someone to procure patients for you'."

Langs commented, "This remark is valuable but let's remember we have to validate it later, through the words of the patient."

Winter proceeded, "After the security guard led the patient to my floor, the patient then asked a doctor in the corridor where my office was."

A psychiatrist said, "That showed his great dependency on other people."

"Do we talk of dependency?" a social worker asked Langs.

"As you seem to know, I never use the word dependency or any other intellectualized term," Langs answered. "It's a wastebasket word. A cliché. When you use a cliché, you obliterate the underlying meanings. I find the word doesn't do anything for me or my patients."

Winter went on, "As the patient walked in, I shook his hand. He said, 'Sorry I got lost. I also forgot to bring the insurance papers'."

The group shook their individual heads sagely, aware of what this meant. Langs put the meaning into words: "He is saying there should be no insurance forms, though consciously he may deny this. He is bringing an encoded message and at the same time giving a model for rectifying—stopping—the damage. He tells you unconsciously through his forgetting that he does not want a third party present during his treatment. He wants his sessions kept confidential. As does every patient."

Winter continued, "After the patient sat down, I asked, 'What seems to be the problem and how can I be of help'?

"The patient said, 'The reason I'm here is that it's part of my condition for parole. I was committed for a violent crime. I was in the joint from 1979 to 1982. When I got out, they told me I had to see somebody like you until you said I didn't need to come any more. So maybe I don't commit another crime.'

"He paused, then said, 'I don't have any problems really. My problem is that one time I committed a crime. I'm here because the parole commissioner said I should come.'" Winter added, to all of us, "The parole commissioner is a woman."

Then he went on, "I said to the patient, 'What did you do that was a crime?' "

He stopped, added swiftly, knowing the group was well aware of Langs' belief that questions by a therapist were, as a rule, inappropriate and tended to interfere with communication between patient and therapist, frightening the patient. "I know I shouldn't have asked this. I think I was feeling rather anxious in the presence of a violent criminal."

A psychologist said reassuringly, "I think we all understand your anxiety. I would be frightened in the presence of a criminal. You're helping me see how questions are designed to protect ourselves from threats by the patient rather than to enhance listening."

Langs remarked to the psychologist, "Your point is well taken. I would have been silent. To intervene here is to act out of your own anxiety, in all likelihood."

Then, to Winter, "It may be that your patient wanted you to be frightened of him. He told you that he's capable of violence, that he broke society's rules in violent fashion. But you must take this as an encoded message. First and foremost, you must formulate the encoded message as a valid perception of *you* in light of your interventions. He seems to be telling you, 'I don't want to be here, it's not my idea, I don't trust you'."

"But isn't the patient also saying something about himself as well?" asked a psychiatrist.

"Every message contains an image of both the therapist and the patient," Langs answered. "But therapists tend to neglect the image of themselves and focus entirely on the image of the patient, which may often be quite secondary, in terms of a deviation. Usually what is more important is the selective image the patient has of you after you intervene. The one meaning he has selected out of the many meanings available."

Langs addressed Winter, "Let's center on your patient's image of you and try to decode what he is saying. When you ask 'What did you do that was a crime'? you're somewhat breaking the ground rules. You're interrupting his thoughts. You're violating his space and his right to tell you about himself in his own pace. Patients prescribe their treatment. You have only to wait and eventually integrate what they can only give you in pieces.

"Each time you intervene, you create a new adaptive context which will generate unconscious perceptions of you to which the patient may add some exaggeration. There will be many rich implications even to the most simple question from a therapist."

A psychologist commented, "It seems to me there's another function of the question Winter asked about what kind of crime the patient committed. It tends to deny the therapist's feelings of criminality, to dump them into the patient, blame him. As I've studied your work, Dr. Langs, it has become clear we do a lot of intervening just to deny our own and the patient's unconscious perceptions of our errors."

A social worker agreed. "It's my impression a question of this kind reflects some problem in the therapist."

Langs said, "In this case, as Winter admitted, he was frightened of the patient's violence, the patient's madness, and responded with anxiety in a self-protective intervention. All too often, the madness of the patient sets off mad reactions, especially mad defenses, in therapists. Our goal is to understand this madness, digest or metabolize it, and interpret it to the patient in terms of his perceptions of our deviations, which seem to him as a kind of madness."

An apologetic look on his face, Winter continued, "The patient said, 'I committed armed robbery and burglary. I did it because I needed the money. This guy and I were sitting at a bar and he's telling me how I can make five hundred dollars real easy. He says, "Come on, Man." He keeps pushing and pushing. So I finally say, "Let's do it." So we broke into a stereo store and stole equipment and beat up the owner. We got caught. I was just stupid'."

One of the psychiatrists said to Winter, "I find his response quite interesting. First, I hear him say you are pushing him. His image of his friend pushing him into crime is a sound unconscious perception of the pressure you created in him with your question about what crime he committed."

Langs said, "That's an excellent point. It's essential we validate our conclusions as well as our interventions."

The psychiatrist continued, "But I also hear of someone who does something dishonest because he needs money. The image of a therapist who is willing to accept a lower fee. It's as if the patient is telling the therapist that he sees him as hungry and greedy and that's why the therapist has accepted him into treatment. I can only suspect that he thinks of his treatment as criminal because the parole board has ordered him to have it. It does not come out of his wish. He is being forced into treatment, punished."

Langs commented, "I'm delighted to hear how well prepared you all are for these listening exercises. I can add a bit. The patient may also be telling Winter that in some way his treatment began in a fashion that duplicated his criminal spree. He was pushed into treatment at a lower fee because he lacked money, with a therapist who also seems to need money.

"There's also images of collusion. For the patient, this may involve the first therapist and Winter, as well as the parole board and both therapists, especially the present one. In this light, the image of being pushed into the crime has to do with the parole board pushing him into treatment, with the therapist as a willing party to this crime."

Langs added, to Winter, "That feeling was compounded when you asked him to reveal himself prematurely. It's important to have faith in the patient. To sit back and let the patient communicate meaning to you in his own time, rather than because of your need to know. In general, this is how we learn valid technique. If your question had been useful, well timed and valid, you would have received positive derivative images. The patient would have talked about a person doing something constructive or how he was in a situation where a question proved helpful.

"But this was not the case. Nor is it typically the case when therapists ask questions. Patients feel they're being put off, blamed, dumped into. Or the surface level is stressed and their unconscious perceptions of the therapist are ignored."

A psychologist said, "The patient also seems to be indicating he is forced to expose himself."

Langs noted, "It is interesting how the patient works over all these deviations on his own terms, in light of his pathology. Another patient might see the experience as a collusion between a mother and father. Or as a type of homosexual seduction. For the moment, this patient sees the collusion in terms of Winter's committing a crime, being dishonest, so that the patient feels entrapped. Deviations create a set of pressures to which the patient responds in terms of his own life experiences."

I started to understand what Langs was saying, that patients respond in terms of their own conflicts and past torments and erotic pleasures and hates but specifically what a patient pulls out of the vast, seething cauldron of instinctual desires is related to something the therapist has said or done. Not one word spoken on the couch or from the chair is *accident*. It is premeditation planned by the unconscious.

At this point Langs spoke a few words about why he considers it essential to listen carefully for the unconscious meaning of what the patient is saying before making an interpretation. He quoted Dr. D. W. Winnicott: "I interpret to let the patient know where my ignorance begins."

Langs explained that a patient dares not tell a therapist, on whom he depends to save his psychic life, that he thinks the therapist is selfish, or disgusting, or stupid, or corrupt, if he answers the telephone in the patient's presence, taking valuable, expensive minutes from his hour. Or attack the therapist if he is ten minutes late. Instead, the patient engages in what Langs describes as a "remarkable capacity" to find an image or story that contains within it the message he wants to convey. He automatically uses the unconscious part of his mind to get across to the therapist the latent or hidden meaning that will reveal his wounded feelings. He resorts to the psychological processes of displacement and symbolization, two of the major ways the unconscious mind works to guard us from inner danger.

In turn, what the therapist expresses to the patient may also contain these unconscious messages, Langs pointed out, even though it is his responsibility to communicate to the patient primarily conscious thoughts. Langs told us, "This is one of the differences in responsibility between patient and therapist. When the therapist makes an error, he shifts to the patient's kind of communication. With the deviant therapist, you find he says one thing but means another. He is not aware of the deeper meaning."

Once again he cautioned, "Remember, every figure, every image, every narrative by the patient essentially represents the therapist and something he has done. First and foremost, we are perceptive human beings — our survival depends on it. Once we perceive, we may exaggerate and it is here the patient's traumatic past comes into play. Freud was right and wrong in his definition of transference. He was right in stating that the relationship between patient and analyst evokes powerful communications relating to the patient's neurosis. He was wrong in saying the patient primarily distorts and transfers. The patient is primarily perceptive but on an unconscious level. Then, and *only* then, does he distort, or more often, simply exaggerate."

Langs pointed out that in Winter's case, the patient's images seemed to show what he felt about Winter, as well as experiences from his past, and that Winter, as he listened, had to ask himself, "What did I do that justifies this as an encoded image of me?" Langs said, "The memories a patient recalls during his first hour are very important. While he is telling you the history of his past and his symptoms, he is already reacting to your interventions, telling you what you have done in error. Your ear should tell you what he is working over. This is the gift a patient bestows on you."

Langs nodded at Winter to go on. Winter said, "I asked the patient, 'Can you tell me a little about your life before this all happened?' And he told me, 'I was doing pretty good. I did good in college. I got through the Army. I had a good job with the state in engineering. But there was this girl and she liked to go out and get high. My money was going to keep her happy.

"'I was married before I went into the Army and sent to Vietnam. I had been going with this other girl and married her three or four months before I went overseas, when she got pregnant. Though I wasn't dying to get married, I figured I would try it and see if it worked out. I made it through Nam and got this job with the state. They gave it back when I got out of the joint. Boy, I know it was stupid to steal that stuff and rough up the owner. My parole officer thinks you might be able to come up with some reason I don't know, other than getting money'."

Again to show how a therapist listens to derivatives, Langs pointed out that the patient's associations revealed he was saying that he was "pregnant" by the therapist, revealing his image of merger, one that takes place in every therapy. It also referred to the merger between the two therapists involved in his treatment and how he felt manipulated by them as he had felt manipulated by his wife into marrying her when she became pregnant.

Winter continued, "I finally made an interpretation to him. I said, 'You have mentioned what happens to you when you feel under pressure. Especially pressure from women. You ended up doing things you're not sure you wanted to do. Like the pressure to get money for your girl friend leading to the robbery. And your wife's forcing you into marriage. And another woman, the parole commissioner, pressuring you to come here'."

Langs said approvingly, "This is, on the whole, a good intervention. We see the therapist eventually alluding to an adaptive context — his involvement with a parole commissioner who is pressuring the patient to go to the therapist. The focus is mainly on the parole officer but there is certainly the implication that the therapist acknowledges his involvement. Here is an intervention alluding to an adaptive context and the derivative communication."

Winter went on, "The patient said, 'Yeah, you may be right. I never thought of it that way. I sure am getting pressure now. Some other woman wants me to move in with her. I'm living with my brother. A man needs to be independent first. I'm doing good and I don't want to give it up to move in with a woman.'

"Then he said, 'It was important to have money for Eva, my girl friend, and that is why I stole. I thought about that in the joint. I stole to keep her happy, and what did I have to show for it? Three years missing out of my life. Three wasted years. With my wife, too.

We got divorced pretty soon after I got back from Nam. She said we didn't have anything in common any more. Nothing to share. She wanted a divorce. So I said "Sure. We can split." But now, when I think about it, I shouldn't have let her go without at least talking to her. I didn't even try to see if there were things I could do to make our life happier. I think I should have hung in there longer'."

Langs commented, "The patient seems to be saying, through encoded messages, that he was seeking therapy under protest, that he had been thinking of leaving treatment after the first hour but on second thought, with the therapist showing he was able to understand the patient's feelings, he thought he might hang in there longer and at least 'talk' to him."

Winter reported that the patient then paused for a long time and finally said, "I don't know what else to tell you. Is it time to go?"

"I said, 'We have a few more minutes'.

"He said, after another pause, 'You know, I've never had any close friends, really. I've had acquaintances but no one close. To talk to. I just never have'."

Langs commented, "At the end of the hour he tells the therapist he is willing to consider that the therapist might be his first close friend. That he is willing to try therapy in spite of all the deviations from the ground rules."

Other cases were presented in which Langs pointed out the therapist's deviations and the group commented on the patient's encoded messages and images of the therapist. At one point Langs said, "Patients want to help you understand them, know the unconscious basis of their illness. Unconsciously, every patient can prescribe the truth. We, as therapists, can only follow the unconscious meaning of what patients are saying to prescribe for them in their own wisdom. They give the derivatives from which you can deduce how you are breaking the rules, threatening the patient's need for what Winnicott called 'holding' and Wilfred Bion called 'containment'. Only as you understand your errors, if you are making them, can you go on to understand and eventually interpret the patient's past traumas and help him achieve insight."

The seminar continued for the next four afternoons as other members presented their cases, which were discussed in the same fashion, showing the therapists' deviations and the patients' unconscious reactions to them as reflected in their words. I did not stay the full week, having other commitments, and feeling I had absorbed all of Langs' teaching I could at one stretch. As one of the psychiatrists said to me, "There are depths to this approach that cannot be reached at once. They are understood only as you experience them over and over. But once you grasp what the approach offers both patient and therapist, you feel committed to it."

Capponi pointed out to me that Langs emphasizes that unless a therapist is analyzed so as to "have the courage and the skills to face painful personal realities, he may say or do something (sometimes remaining silent when the need is for him to make an interpretation, or make an interpretation when it is not warranted) which, instead of helping the patient work over his problems, will direct him to turn away and close up that part of his life again.

"To become aware of this is painful for us. We are honestly, and to the best of our talents, trying to fulfill our responsibility to help our patients and it is discouraging to realize that we have to learn new things and change some of our old ways of working. This is why more young and beginning therapists are attracted to Langs. They have less to unlearn and suffer less narcissistic injuries.

"You remember in Sophocles' *Oedipus Rex* that Tiresias tells King Oedipus he is better off not knowing the truth. But he insists on knowing the truth at any cost and as the truth gradually unravels, the reader begins to experience the King's terror. If therapy keeps going on and on without any moments of terror for both therapist and patient, it is because Tiresias has prevailed."

Capponi believes that "when you catch on to what Langs is saying, it's breathtaking." Capponi thinks Langs is the first analyst in years to apply one of Freud's basic concepts in a creative way to the material of a session, putting the therapist as well as the patient at the heart of the psychoanalytic process. Freud built a psychology and therapy based on the understanding of the unconscious part of the mind and its processes. But many therapists have been as frightened of the unconscious as their patients are, and have turned away from it in a clinical sense, though they may write of its power in an intellectual sense, Capponi asserted.

He said what he found new in Langs was a different way of

listening that revealed the patient constantly monitors the therapist's words, tone of speech and acts, and communicates their effects. This listening applies particularly to the patient's reactions when a ground rule is broken.

One thing Langs emphasizes, perhaps more than any other therapist, Capponi says, is the role of the ground rules in providing the conditions necessary for the psychoanalytic therapeutic process to take place. He adds, "This is not a new idea, except that Langs is consistently more concerned about it and shows what the consequences are when you modify the ground rules for unconsciously or consciously convenient reasons. Therapy, to me, is like the process of gestation. You need a steady state for a given period of time. When you change one condition, you disturb the process and you don't get a normal organism. Or, in the case of therapy, an effective outcome."

As I headed back to Manhattan, I decided to read more of what Langs had written about the listening process and the importance of ground rules. One psychic step at a time, like in analysis, where, if you try to understand everything at once, you understand nothing. But if you understand one fantasy and the wish behind it, unconscious repercussions produce internal change, like a psychic pebble tossed into the dark depths of the mind.

3
THE ARTFUL
LISTENER

Langs had gratified for a few days my wish to be a therapist. When I graduated from Bennington College I had been torn between becoming a social worker or journalist and though writing won out, the wish to help the troubled never vanished (mirroring, as I later learned in analysis, my own wish to be helped).

I telephoned Langs to thank him for the chance to sit in at the supervision sessions and asked if he would give me an appointment to answer questions about the listening process. He set a time.

Three days later as I walked the four blocks to his midtown office, I thought how important listening is in our lives. We all need someone who listens, especially when we feel troubled. To be heard is an early vital need, shown in the cry of the baby who counts on his mother's listening to bring her to his side when he is hungry or cold or in pain from some hurt. The growing child needs his mother to listen to his first words, to encourage him to talk, to learn, to seek independence.

But after we grow up, it often seems as though no one really listens, either to our spoken or unspoken pleas. If we feel unhappy and can afford it, we may pay a therapist to satisfy the inner, gnawing need to be heard. Therapy eases inner agony through the therapist's ability to listen. Of words heard, and then through the use of the therapist's own words, come the interpretations that bring us new awareness of the unrealistic fantasies and wishes causing unhappiness.

Seated in a comfortable black fabric-covered chair next to a small table, I faced Langs, who sat in a brown plaid chair to the right of the head of the couch, a muted orange shade. Langs answers questions graciously, a natural teacher. Even a simple question like the one I threw at him first, simple for him since he had written extensively on the subject in *The Listening Process:* "Can you briefly explain your special listening process?"

"The listening process is where I started and it has been the means of reaching further discoveries," he said. "I believe that listening, in the true therapeutic sense, has but one meaning. Hearing the patient's encoded message and learning the stimulus that triggered it — the interventions of the therapist. Only the therapist who reaches awareness of the stimulus is experienced by the patient as 'listening'. The only time a patient feels he has been heard is when his unconscious message is decoded."

"Don't all analysts do this?" I asked.

"The interpretations that a number of analysts give are merely inferences based on the patient's conscious thoughts," he said. "These interpretations do not take into consideration the patient's encoded message, one that focuses on the interaction between himself and the analyst."

I thought, He is saying that all too often the analyst fails to listen with that "third ear" Theodor Reik mentioned; perhaps there is sad truth in that old joke about the young analyst in training who asks his supervisor, "How can you bear to listen to such agonizing life stories hour after hour?" and receives the response, "Who listens?" At least not in Langs' fashion.

He was saying, "Once I started to listen to patients I heard material I never imagined existed. My Rosetta stone was the concept that a patient adaptively responded to the interventions of the therapist. I found the interventions, which included not only interpretations but also silences and any behavior that affected the relationship to the patient in the slightest degree, were loaded with the errors and pathology of the therapist."

He went on, "Even more surprising, I discovered that a patient's perceptions had a keen, displaced, encoded sensitivity to the erroneous interventions of the therapist. Perceptions that arose out of the richness of the unconscious part of the patient's mind. These perceptions are revealed in the messages the analyst has to decode."

To understand the decoding, Langs explained, is to understand, first, that there are two ways we communicate with another person. One is the "single message unit." This occurs when we say exactly what we mean — when we give directions, lecture or teach. The other is the "multiple message unit" — we say one thing but conceal in it a second message.

There is a multiple message, for instance, in every dream. A dream holds a disguised message to the self which needs to be decoded according to the language of the unconscious processes of the mind. We also use the multiple message when we do not wish to tell other people directly how we feel, or what we think, because we might lose their love or respect or spark their anger. We are not aware we give these hidden messages which we deliver unconsciously, automatically. We are compelled to give them, we cannot stop giving them, because it is psychologically painful to hold them back.

Langs explained, "A patient in therapy talks on one level, what therapists call the manifest or surface level. But his words contain the message he is hiding from the therapist and himself. The therapist knows, or should know, that the multiple message communication is a safety valve for the patient. It represents partial discharge in disguised form of thoughts in him that are creating intolerable tension. The multiple message is one of the ingenious ways the unconscious part of our mind works to preserve our sanity. Quite often the message relates to something the therapist has done to hurt or anger the patient."

Langs gave as illustration a therapist who had changed a female patient's regular 10 A.M. hour to 4 P.M. so he could give the earlier hour to a male patient unable to arrange any other time. She said angrily during her first session at the new hour, "My father always kept me waiting when we were to meet. He wasn't fair, he didn't consider my feelings." She was giving the therapist the message, as she displaced her feelings from him to her father, "You keep me waiting until later in the day for my appointment, you are not fair, and I am very angry."

Langs commented, "She had a right to be angry. The therapist who changes a patient's regular hour to suit his economic need is attacking, not supporting, that patient. This woman told her therapist in her encoded message how outraged she felt. Until he understood this, and realized his act had been hostile, she will remain furious."

Langs said that as he first began to decode hidden messages from patients, he found the patients unconsciously related with positive images to good interventions by the therapists. But when the therapist made an error in interpretation or broke a ground rule, the patient, on an unconscious level, communicated a negative image of the therapist.

Langs kept decoding communications of patient after patient, listening to what Freud called "derivatives." A derivative is a surface message that contains an encoded meaning—the expression of unconscious perceptions about the therapist. By decoding the message, the therapist learns what Langs calls the "adaptive context" that has influenced the patient's conscious and unconscious thoughts.

"The way most therapists listen to a patient is based not on understanding the unconscious and conscious communication between patient and analyst during what Dr. Thomas Szasz has described as 'a unique dialogue,' but on the conscious communication alone," Langs said. "If a patient's conscious thoughts were all, the patient would not need therapy. The analyst must be aware not only of the *conscious* free associations but also of what the patient tells him indirectly through displacement onto someone else. Displacement is one of our strong defensive psychological processes. Patients resort to it especially when ground rules are broken."

The warning that therapists must constantly try to be aware of their unconscious feelings toward a patient, particularly the hostile and erotic ones, has been stated in articles by classical psychoanalysts but never in connection with the breaking of ground rules, Langs pointed out.

"I believe I have added a new level to the process of psychoanalysis," he said. "Just as I believe further levels will be added by others in years to come." He described himself as "the eternal patient." He believes every therapist should be the eternal patient, not only to help the patient more effectively but to advance the knowledge of the human mind.

To do both, the therapist must work on awareness of what goes on in the unconscious part of his mind, decoding his hidden messages to himself and, at the same time, decoding hidden messages the patient is sending him.

For a number of psychoanalysts this may be difficult, Langs maintains, for they are "fixated at the level of knowledge at which they were graduated from a psychoanalytic institute, it is a great struggle to get beyond that. Analysts are also fixated, I think, at the level at which their own analysts were functioning. It takes a lot of personal self analysis or a second or third analysis to change further."

Therapists tend to stay with known principles embodied in their training as a way of managing anxieties and maintaining a false sense of security, Langs said. This often leads them to "develop forced formulations based more on accepted but erroneous theory than on a sensitive listening to the material from the patient."

Freud created difficulties, Langs believes, by initially writing about the unconscious part of the mind, which is an abstraction, as though it substantially existed. Often analysts call it "the unconscious" as if it were a thing or place. Instead, Langs thinks of it, as Freud later described it, as a quality of certain types of mental functioning, of thoughts and feelings outside direct awareness. One way this type of mental functioning acts in behalf of self preservation is to disguise, through displacement or the use of a symbol, our communication of an image that is dangerous or threatening. What Langs calls a "raw" image, or any fantasy or perception that brings mental distress.

"What percentage of therapists listen the way you do?" I asked.

"A number of psychoanalysts. It's mainly therapists who are not trained in the classical method, who do not understand the concept or functions of the unconscious part of the mind, who don't listen properly," he said. "A large part of ineffective therapy is derived from a basic failure among psychotherapists to develop a comprehensive capacity for listening and validating in the true psychoanalytic sense.

"Listening is our basic tool, and the listener, our basic instrument. We must be open to all avenues of communication from the patient, regardless of the techniques we choose to practice. We must hear manifest messages, of course, but we must then reach into their unconscious meanings so we understand their latent, derivative or encoded messages. It is remarkable there are so few papers on the listening process. The therapist is permitted to listen 'with a tin ear,' as it were."

Both patient and therapist have a responsibility in the important act of listening, Langs believes. The patient's responsibility is to talk freely and convey unconscious messages. The therapist's responsibility is to decode the messages.

The therapist must know what the patient is communicating in encoded fashion about the therapist before he can give helpful interpretations, as Langs told the Long Island group. If the therapist interprets only on the basis of unconscious implications as they relate to the earlier life of the patient, leaving out the therapist's own acts and words as the trigger, then the therapist is missing the essential quality of the treatment.

Langs calls any intervention made by a therapist without awareness of this interaction "lie therapy" — a falsification. The therapist consistently avoids acknowledging a contribution to the patient's symptoms, communications and therapeutic experience and thereby "falsifies" the true meaning of the patient's associations. Whereas in "truth therapy" therapists are aware of what they may be doing or saying to arouse anxiety, anger or fear in patients.

The patient is the therapist's "best supervisor," though the patient's efforts are chiefly unconscious. Langs explains: "The therapist has to know how to appreciate what the patient is communicating. Both patient and therapist are always communicating — both intrapsychically and interactionally. For the therapist, this process is generated by his openness to receive as well as organize and by the patient's efforts, usually unconscious, to have the therapist experience certain images and thoughts."

The patient can facilitate or interfere with the therapist's capacity to listen, just as the therapist's own emotional conflicts may impair what Langs calls the "listening capacity." He maintains that "listening," in analytic psychotherapy, "means being open to chaos and uncertainty, being constantly receptive and sensitive, but it also means knowing how to organize the patient's material and how to understand it. The listening process determines the therapist's interpretation and its timing. It covers everything the therapist does, or is, at least, essential to all he does. It culminates in the formulation of an interpretation."

The therapist uses the therapeutic relationship as the basis of understanding the patient's inner conflicts, and every session, from the first to the last, should be considered the interactional product of both patient and analyst, Langs insists. The patient is consciously and unconsciously concerned with, and reacting to, the therapist all the time, *without exception*, according to Langs. The patient's outside relationships, which may cause trauma and evoke important unconscious communications to the point where they should be interpreted, will, by and large, be secondary. When they become central, they still hold an important link to the relationship with the therapist.

"All communications from the patient are adaptively determined and organized," Langs said. "All experiences with the analyst impinge on the psyche of the patient as he keeps working them over both consciously and unconsciously. The proper understanding of this working over process relates to the hidden message contained in the patient's words, stimulated by the adaptive context."

Langs' concept of the adaptive context came out of his realization of the relationship between what Freud called "the day residue" and the dream. Langs calls the day residue and the dream "the model for all mental functioning, the interplay between reality and fantasy."

The day residue refers to something we see or think or are confronted with during the day that sparks our perceptions, fantasies and memories which appear in disguised form in that night's dream. No dream exists without day residue. The latter is the key to the dream — both its stimulant and organizer. It structures the story and images of the dream, calls forth the disguises of displacement, symbolism, distortion, the use of the part for the whole, and other defenses of the unconscious part of the mind that must be understood before the true meaning of the dream emerges.

In the same way therapists analyze dreams, they learn the adaptive context that governs what patients unconsciously say to them in sessions. Unless therapists understand this adaptive context, they are not listening in a psychoanalytic sense, and the patients will be burdened with the therapists' errors, defenses and pathology, Langs maintains.

An adaptive context has two effects, both communicative, according to Langs: "One is a symptom and the other is a more clearly encoded message. Symptoms, such as a headache or nervous coughs or sighs, are encoded messages but they yield little clear meaning. On the other hand, derivatives are messages that create a great deal of meaning. If we know the adaptive context, with its implications, we can use the derivative material, what I call the 'derivative complex', as a way of understanding the unconscious meanings of the patient's symptoms and emotional illness. The same stimulus has led to a symptomatic response and a message response, and the two are equivalent.

"The study of the psychoanalytic literature shows that therapists, for the most part, ignore the adaptive context. They do not decode the unconscious messages of patients and thus do not understand their own contributions to the patient's disturbances. Therapists who keep patients waiting, or make critical remarks, are ignoring their own behavior and the angry reactions it will bring from patients."

"Everything the therapist does — silences, questions, clarifications, confrontations, interpretations or reconstruction of the patient's past — should involve an awareness of the particular adaptive context of the moment," Langs said. "The therapist is responsible for listening to the free associations that indicate the context without allowing his subjective intrusions to disturb the listening process to the point he does not 'hear' the patient."

The therapist should clarify to himself both his own and the patient's contributions to each session. The therapist should recognize which of his responses are, in Langs' words, "empathic, intuitive and understanding," and which are "essentially pathological and distorting." He also "must try to identify with the patient, empathize with him, and imagine how he will process what has been communicated to him or interactionally placed into him."

Langs described a case he supervised in which a psychologist was seeing a depressed forty-year-old female patient who remained in a marriage she considered a torture. In this particular session she entered the office looking upset, promptly told the psychologist she thought he was "cruel" because he had said not a word during her previous session.

Approaching the end of the session, she burst into tears. She then took a piece of Kleenex out of her purse and wiped away the tears. The psychologist stood up, walked behind his desk to hand her an appointment slip for her next hour. Suddenly he said, "A piece of Kleenex is sticking to your face."

She wiped it off. Then she rushed around the desk, clasped his hands tightly and implored him to please tell her in the next session why he was so silent during her therapy. She let go his hands, apologized in a somewhat sarcastic tone for touching him and swept out of the office.

Langs pointed out the psychologist had broken a ground rule in making a "non-neutral" intervention. He had told the patient a piece of Kleenex was attached to her face, paying her undue personal attention. It was this seductive act that led to her impulsive, seductive wish to rush over and grasp his hands, knowing the touch was forbidden.

"To understand the patient's inner world and empathize does not imply that the therapist behave in a way that confirms that inner world," Langs said. "A valid understanding of that inner world, especially of its pathological components, requires that the therapist behave in a manner distinctly different from the pathological aspects of that inner world and its past, pathogenic figures." This therapist had behaved as the patient's father once behaved (he had called her a "sloppy, messy little girl"). The therapist's comment threw her into the panic that drove her to clasp his hands as though to get close to him and have him reassure her she was a very orderly, clean little girl.

The therapist's words were manipulative and seductive, Langs said. They also reflected a sense of helplessness in him: "It's a rather naive appeal to the patient to be a good patient, to work with the therapist, not give him a hard time. Unconsciously, the patient hears this message and its influence will be reflected in her communications in the following hour."

When she returned for the next session, she accused the therapist of being brutal and threatened to stop therapy because she could not bear further suffering. Then, in contradiction, she begged him to speak more often, saying she could not stand his silence.

"When a therapist intervenes noninterpretatively, as in this case, when he mentioned the Kleenex, he arouses the patient's anxiety," Langs explained. "He intervened for his sake, not the patient's."

The psychologist had defended himself by explaining he had pointed out the piece of Kleenex so the woman would not be embarrassed when she walked out into the street. Langs told the psychologist he was upset because the patient had probably awakened his memories of not wishing to be a "messy, dirty little boy," fearing a scolding from his parents. He had allowed the patient to take his hands as he, when a little boy, had wanted the physical assurance he was loved even though dirty. He should have refused to let the patient touch him, then analyzed her wish to do so at the next session.

The psychologist's behavior, Langs explained, intended as encouragement and reassurance to the patient, unconsciously constitutes a threat. It discourages the patient's efforts to communicate, as well as being an unconscious attempt to seduce and to set aside her defenses. The therapist had felt a sense of helplessness, of not being able to contain within himself the devaluation of himself as a boy, which she had unconsciously provoked.

What Langs next said is one of his important tenets: "Unless the therapist is as sensitive to his own pathological reactions as he is to the patient's pathology and the pathological interactional mechanisms, he will be disruptive to treatment. But if a therapist is aware of what the patient is saying in relation to what the therapist has done to hurt or antagonize, this will very quickly place the therapist in touch with the unconscious processes and communications from the patient. While the procedure of decoding creates a considerable conscious burden, therapists will find that any failure to accept and contain that burden, or to metabolize it toward effective therapy, will make it impossible for them to help the patient."

Langs will not, incidentally, use material relating to his own patients. When he first started to write, occasionally he cited a highly disguised vignette from his clinical work. But patients read his books and quickly picked out the case that referred to them, letting him know he had broken the promise of confidentiality, damaged a basic trust. They experienced him as hurtful and rejecting and the therapeutic outcome was compromised.

"So I stopped using my patients as cases," he explained. "There was no choice. My first and most fundamental commitment as a therapist is to my patients. I would never knowingly do anything to harm them or impair the therapeutic setting they need for an effective cure. I firmly decided never again to make use of the material from my patients except for interpretative work in their private sessions." He now uses only material from supervision, where cases are discussed for the purpose of instruction, and even then he disguises the case.

Many therapists in the past believed that the patient's words, to which they listen carefully, have no meaning in terms of the therapist but only reflect the patient's childhood fantasies and his unconscious identification with his mother and father, his early models. "I have not discarded the role of genetics, of early childhood interactions as they contribute to distortion," Langs says. "What I disagree with is that these formulations are used as a barrier to perceptions rather than developing formulations that begin as perceptions. Recognizing, of course, that perceptions sometimes — I want to emphasize this — *sometimes* get distorted."

Only after considering what the therapist might be doing to harm the patient, if the patient's words indicate on an unconscious level this is so, can the therapist turn to the next step of sorting out from the patient's associations those that are valid, based on reality, from those springing out of fantasy and distortion. This means, Langs says, that the listening process must address both reality and fantasy, that it is not, as many therapists believe, "simply a matter of investigating fantasied contents and deriving from them the underlying unconscious fantasies and memories." He describes the basic attitude in listening as "essentially neutral" in that it permits "formulations of both reality and fantasy, and their interplay."

Inherent to the listening process is the therapist's capacity to relate to reality, "on an awareness, first, of his personal standards and guides to reality, and on his ability to resolve, as far as possible, any propensities toward distortions, and secondly, on his capacity for self-knowledge."

The effective therapist, the one who knows reality *and* realizes the patient's perception of it, can help the patient with the crucial functions of testing reality, functioning in reality, appraising reality and differentiating reality from fantasy, all relating to neurosis. Therapists must not only fully understand the implications of external reality but also — their greatest responsibility — inner reality.

I wondered how much of his inner reality one of my therapists had understood. He had never married and when I asked why, he answered, "I felt a greater need to be alone," then added, "He travels fastest who travels alone." From what I was now learning from Langs, this therapist should not have answered my question, much less with clichés. Obviously he had not married because of his fear of and anger at women. When I saw him several years after therapy, he told me his mother had wanted him to be a minister.

Langs believes a number of male therapists have not faced their unconscious hostility to women and their own seductiveness used as defense against the hostility. He cited the case of a female patient who started a series of affairs even though her male therapist advised her not to act on her sexual desire but to analyze it. He had allowed her to accumulate a bill of three months after she said she was temporarily strapped for funds. In her acting out with other men, she was unconsciously telling him he was acting seductively towards her by treating her for no fee.

"Patients unconsciously perceive a therapist's seductiveness," Langs said. "I think most therapists, including a number of psychoanalysts, have underestimated the perceptiveness of their patients. A therapist is not very sensitive if he tells a patient who is promiscuous that her current affairs stem from her seductive relationship with her father. The therapist is overlooking the fact that he may have been promiscuous in some symbolic way. Allowing her to run up bills or to stay overtime if she seemed in the middle of a crisis."

He cited psychoanalyst Margaret Little in an article in 1951 as pointing out when a therapist interprets a patient's associations and reactions only as related to childhood, "you deny their reality; you deny that you have actually behaved in the way that the patient is representing you, and when in error, greatly disturb the patient's capacities for reality-testing — and sometimes even drive the patient crazy."

Therapists tend to deny the patient's conscious feelings about them and to ignore the patient's unconscious feelings about them, Langs said. He cited the example of one therapist who told a patient her feeling that he was critical was based on the way she felt as a child toward a father who criticized her constantly. The patient then spoke of her boyfriend as highly critical of what she wore. She was telling her therapist on an unconscious level that she felt he was indeed critical, no matter how strongly he denied it.

Langs said, "It's a rather undemocratic characteristic of psychotherapy to suggest the patient speaks on a surface level but the real meaning lies in the unconscious realm, while the therapist talks only on a conscious level—his unconscious messages do not exist. Or, to put it another way, that the therapist is the healthy one and only rarely pathological, while the patient is the sick one, and only rarely, if ever, well. The fair and honest view acknowledges and attempts to sort out the conscious and unconscious communications from the therapist *and* the patient. Such a view addresses them both without prejudice and listens impartially to both."

Langs tells the therapists he supervises: "I'm trying to teach you that if you are honest you're going to explore the whole world of your unconscious intentions and emotions, most of which are unpleasant for you to confront. But you have to know this world if you're going to be able to appreciate what your patient is perceiving and feeling, and understand the real factors in his pathology—if you're going to do valid psychotherapy."

Dr. Paul Gray in "'Developmental Lag' in Technique," published in the *Journal of the American Psychoanalytic Association,* 1982, says, "It is difficult for analysts to overcome narcissistic self-protection against having their actual characteristics—appearance, ways of speaking, ways of thinking (as these become apparent), etc.—accurately perceived by the patient as a part of effective analytic process."

Gray describes what he calls the developmental lag in technique as occurring because analysts have failed to assimilate and apply information acquired about the importance of the ego in therapeutic effectiveness. He believes too many analysts still concentrate on the reconstruction of past experiences and the strong id drives rather than help the patient face and understand his resistances to knowing the truth and also, in Freud's phrase, the "resistances to uncovering resistances." Gray calls such an approach the analysis of "defense before drive."

He says the argument made in behalf of analyzing the drives rather than the defenses erected against expressing them fails to recognize that to observe a defense — much less to demonstrate its existence and motive to the analysand — is, with rare exception, not possible without having perceived and noted to the patient the "id derivative against which it is directed." He quotes Dr. Leo Stone as referring to "the strange magnetism which the verbal statement of unconscious content exerts on analysts."

Discussing what he calls the resistances to analyzing ego defenses in the face of certain burdensome consequences to the analyst, Gray lists four "so designated fixations." The first is fascination with the id; the second, predilection for an authoritative analytic stance; the third, preoccupation with external reality, including the past as external reality; and the fourth, counter-resistance to transference emotions and impulses.

Gray says it is especially *"because* the patient's 'real' perceptions of the analyst will be *included* in the material [that the patient provides if his defenses are examined], particularly as defenses against the act of perception are worked through, that the analyst's counter-resistance to observing and analyzing the ego's activities is easily aroused."

As I read Gray's article I was reminded of a passage in a personal letter from Paul Koseleff, a Danish psychologist, referring to a defense. Koseleff wrote, "One stands in awe of a child's achievements, they are brilliant works of art. The baby and the child solve problems with regard to all kinds of behavior in order both to manage the social demands and pressures, often harsh ones, and to satisfy as many as possible of their own needs and desires. The child must manage to steer clear of Scylla and the Sirens, it must make its own charts, it must avoid bumping against hard obstacles and the monsters' sharp teeth. Though the charts and the compass must be corrected and adjusted, the child does this with artistry." He was saying the defenses we erect against our pain are to be admired and, in therapy, to be carefully observed by the therapist, who helps us understand why we erect them and then to face the inner pain the defense protected us against. If I had to select one thing in my many years of analysis that infuriated me the most it was the indelicate, sometimes cruel way an analyst would point out a defense, as though it were something bad I had done, not at that moment seeing the torment it hid. Perhaps one reason analysts have been slow to take hold of the ego approach, which is so concerned with defenses, is because to be effective, ego psychology requires a particularly sensitive, compassionate analyst with a knowledge of timing. As the Bible says, there is a time for everything — including the unveiling of a defense. There is also the possibility, as some analysts believe, that as the underlying traumas are faced, the defenses automatically fall, no longer needed.

Therapists' self-knowledge, their capacity to test reality, but especially their ability to understand their own unconscious communications to patients are the backdrop for every aspect of the listening process, Langs believes. These qualities are relevant in sorting out both the realistic and the distorted aspects of the patient's communications. Not only in relation to the content but for the understanding by the therapist of the nature of the patient's defenses and the extent to which they are appropriate and nonneurotic or inappropriate and pathological.

"Any last words on 'listening'?" I asked Langs, as I prepared to leave.

He suggested, "The therapist as he listens should think in terms of images, fantasies and perceptions. Efforts at formulating the patient's material should be essentially devoid of theoretical concepts and intellectualized inferences. Instead, the therapist should operate as if writing a novel or a play — think of scenes, images, human emotions, human conflict and struggle. In substance, this is the language of unconscious expression and communication."

Extended narratives with rich imagery, whether the recall of recent or past events in the form of a dream or conscious fantasy, tend to be strong potential carriers from the patient of encoded messages, Langs said. Whereas direct comments about the therapist, attempts by the patient at interpreting his own dreams or other material, direct complaints about therapy or conscious praise of the therapist, discussions of how therapy works, speculations about other people, and behavioral and somatic responses are poor carriers of encoded messages.

I thanked Langs, gathered up my notes, started the walk home. I summed up his prime message in listening: the therapist, in hearing the patient's words, must relate them not only to the patient's past, but to what the therapist has said or done to which the patient is unconsciously reacting. The therapist's communications to the patient have unconscious contents despite the therapist's wish to communicate primarily on the conscious level. The therapist must try to know his unconscious thoughts and feelings and how they may be affecting the patient's trust so the therapy is disrupted. All the intellectual interpretations in the world will not help a patient who is confused by divided meanings in the therapist's interventions as he says one thing but means another — which the patient will sense.

Langs is saying to therapists that if they want to cure patients, they have to know the truth about themselves. Therapists should listen carefully not only to what the patients say unconsciously but to their own inner voices.

Langs' words as I left his office rang in my ears. He had said, "It is the nature of therapy that a therapist will never be fully at peace with his work."

Are any of us ever "fully at peace" with work or life, I wondered, isn't such a wish one more fantasy of perfection, the perfection we demanded as a child from what seemed our magical parents, and the perfection we demand as adults from our therapists? The analyst is not the God we dreamed him to be, he is only another human being, but one with the patience and ability to draw out memories wound round with wild fantasies and help us view them with the eyes of maturity.

It is unrealistic to expect every psychoanalyst to be fully effective. As in any profession, you will find the highly gifted and skillful, then a number not quite so effective, then others less effective. Analytic work has particular hazards, both physical and psychological. What other professional sits quietly in a chair all the hours of a working day listening to various patients speak of their misery, woes and rage? To help patients the analyst has to develop a self-control and an awareness of both self and the patient that is herculean. The work of understanding the self goes on for a lifetime in both patient and analyst.

4
THE SACROSANCT
BOUNDARIES

What Langs calls the "listening process" reveals the breaking of a ground rule by the therapist. But say you had that perfect therapist. He would never break a ground rule so there would be no "adaptive context" to enrage the patient and no message to decode, telling of the patient's hurt and anger.

The listening process, however, also applies to every interpretation the therapist makes. From the patient's validations, which include approval in some form — through free associations, dreams, slips of the tongue — the therapist knows the interpretation has been right on target and the patient will benefit from using the therapist's words consciously and unconsciously. If the patient does not validate the interpretation, he has not accepted it.

The belief there is a single, ideal therapeutic setting within which effective interpretations take place is controversial. Many psychoanalysts think certain ground rules can be broken without harm to the patient if the breaks are fully discussed with the patient. But adherence to ground rules appears to have withstood all challenges and offers the best conditions of treatment, Langs claims.

What are called the ground rules of therapy set the scene for the relatedness that gives therapy its distinctive properties — its quota of frustrations and gratifications. And yet the keeping of ground rules "is among the most neglected aspects of psychotherapy," Langs charges. He calls this unfortunate because any break in the rules, he says, "will critically harm the patient's chance at cure."

He suggests "massive research" on the way therapists, especially those conducting nonanalytic therapy, are breaking the ground rules in hostile and seductive ways. He asserts, "The therapist who deviates is saying to the patient, 'I'll never do it right, I'll keep on breaking one ground rule after another, it will be difficult for you here'. The

patient knows this but outwardly accepts the pathological gratification of the break as he feels indulged, merged with the therapist,
plunged into childhood dependency."

Langs emphasizes that the breaking of ground rules encourages
the expression of psychopathology in both patient and analyst. He
says there is an inevitable or inherent need in both for alterations
of the boundaries, "for the pathological symbiotic gratification and
defenses it affords."

It is the therapist's responsibility to know the ground rules and
see they are kept. Most patients do not know ground rules exist,
much less what they are. In all my years of analysis, I was never
conscious of a "ground rule." Though I knew I felt hurt and angry
when an appointment was broken, or the few times a therapist "forgot" my hour and gave it to someone else and we both showed up,
or the answering of the telephone by the therapist as I was in the
middle of some traumatic account.

All patients know is the hurt, confusion, suspicion and anger
they feel when the therapist answers the telephone or cancels an appointment or forgets one. Or when the therapist displays family photographs in the office. Or talks of personal memories. Or speaks
in an irritated tone. Or acts seductively. Or gives advice.

Freud set the initial ground rules. The patient had to lie on the
couch as the analyst sat slightly behind. The patient followed the
command to say everything that came to mind. There was a set fee,
a regular hour five or six days a week. The analysis lasted for a specific length of time which could be prolonged if the patient wished
and the analyst acquiesced.

Other ground rules developed as Freud analyzed more patients.
The patient was not permitted to call the analyst by his first name
nor did the analyst address the patient by his first name. Sessions
could be broken only in emergencies by either analyst or patient.
The analyst was not supposed to bring up anything about his personal life or see the patient outside of the consultation room.

Though Freud set the basic ground rules, at times he permitted himself to break some. He treated husband and wife, in the case
of Alix and James Strachey, who later became his English transla-
tors. Freud accepted his daughter Anna as patient though no ana-

lyst is supposed to treat a relative. He took gifts from patients when the analysis ended because, he said, it made separation easier for the patient.

"Freud showed a distinct laxity in his application of some ground rules, as have many analysts," Langs says. "But Freud had the genius to define a set of valid ground rules and boundaries for the psychoanalytic experience, which he knew should be observed."

A number of psychoanalysts have been analyzed at institutes under conditions in which ground rules were broken, Langs says, adding, "I think this in part accounts for the extensive blind spot in regard to the meaning of ground rules. I cautiously modified some at first because my analyst did, and it was what I had been taught by my superiors. But once I learned how to listen to derivatives, my patients taught me of the damage I was inflicting on them when I broke a rule."

Langs has found patients "exquisitely sensitive to the most minimal deviation in the therapeutic frame. Their responses to such deviations are powerful and universal. The responses are shaped by the specific nature of the deviation, the unconscious communication from the therapist which the deviation implies, and the patient's own inner needs."

Following any break in ground rules, the patient will be working it over in his mind during separation from the therapist and will present his reactions in the next session. If the therapist denies making a break, is not aware of it, does not correct it, and does not understand the patient's reactions in light of the break, the patient will feel betrayed, resentful and angry. But if the therapist understands the nature of the break, intervenes and rectifies it, the patient feels understood and grateful.

The therapist should be sensitive to all important deviations, Langs says, "otherwise a patient will hate him for arousing feelings of insecurity and anxiety. When a therapist makes an error, he must understand why he has felt the need to do so in order that he does not keep on making it. One deviation begets another — what I call Langs' law."

While a patient may consciously welcome a break, unconsciously he will reveal anger and other feelings in perceptions of the analyst. "What typically happens after a break in ground rules is that the patient directly says, 'Thank you,' as though welcoming the break," explains Langs, "but if you listen to his free associations you hear of someone who is trying to overwhelm, corner or destroy him. In some fashion, boundaries are not being maintained. Too few therapists relate this to altered ground rules."

The most important ground rule is that there be a stable, single, relatively neutral setting — an impersonal secure place within which treatment can unfold. This means that the therapist's home or a shared office is not advisable, Langs says. The distractions in such locales interfere with the patient's right to privacy and arouse his hostility. Freud recognized this. His office was never within his home though it was in the same building. Until 1907 he saw patients in an office on the floor below his apartment and from then on, until he left Vienna in 1938, his office was in a separate apartment across the hall from where he lived.

One therapist changed his office from a room in a professional building to the living room of his home. This aroused in his patients the images of being in their parents' bedroom and observing the primal scene, unconscious participation in incest, and other disturbing images, Langs noted. Another therapist shared an office with her husband, a physician, whom her patients often saw enter and leave. Such scenes produce in patients feelings of fear, anger and confusion that permeate the entire therapy.

A second important ground rule, Langs says, is the setting of a single fee which affords the therapist "an important measure of gratification and appropriate reward for his services, and precludes any image of either undue sacrifice or exploitation of the patient. It is necessary the fee be commensurate with the therapist's level of expertise and with fees charged within the community."

Other basic ground rules:

1. A specific and set time for each session, with a defined length for each hour, preferably forty-five or fifty minutes.

2. A full sense of responsibility for attendance at all scheduled sessions on the part of both patient and therapist. The patient is responsible for all sessions for which the thera-

pist is available, and a reasonable vacation policy is set by the therapist, to which both patient and therapist must adhere.

3. The sessions should take place in the therapist's consultation room, which must be suitably soundproofed, as the therapist sits in his chair and the patient sits in another chair or lies on the couch. The office that lacks basic soundproofing is a "vested interest deviation" (Langs' phrase). It is the result of an alteration in the ideal ground rules in that "leakage of sound impairs the communicative qualities of the therapeutic interaction, tends to establish a parasitic mode of relatedness between the patient and therapist (with the patient as the main victim) and generates a highly mistrustful and threatening image of the therapist. The deviation indicates to the patient that it is unsafe to communicate meaningfully to the therapist on a conscious as well as unconscious level." The patient on the chair or couch is aware the patient in the waiting room may hear his words, as he has heard the words of the preceding patient.

4. The fundamental rule of free association must hold, in which the patient expresses to the therapist everything that comes to mind—thoughts, feelings, images—no matter how they reflect on his self-esteem or insult the therapist.

5. The therapist must maintain what Freud called "free-floating attention," open to all the subtle implications of what the patient says in terms of his life and relation to the therapist. The therapist's manner and attitude, reflected in the nature of the therapist's interventions, provide unconscious support for the free associations of the patient.

6. The therapist must keep relative anonymity by avoiding all deliberate self-revelations. The patient experiences revelations by the therapist about himself as pathologically exhibitionistic, an unnecessary confession that lowers respect for the therapist. By withholding information about the self, the therapist not only provides full opportunity for projection by the patient (the process by which the patient

displaces feelings of childhood onto the therapist) but also a sense of safety to the therapeutic relationship. Anonymity on the part of the therapist also reflects willingness "to forego and renounce pathological needs and to repel any tendency to misuse the relationship with the patient for pathological satisfactions," Langs says. He refers not only to outright sexual intimacy or hostile outbreaks but an undercurrent of anger or seductiveness that is not expressed but felt by the patient as surely as any act.

7. The therapist should use valid, neutral active interventions. Interventions should be confined to interpretations and reconstructions (experiences of the past brought to memory) and their variations, and the handling of the ground rules, at the behest of the patient's derivative communications. Here, too, Langs says, the therapist expresses a commitment to the the therapeutic needs of the patient and renounces any pathological use of the treatment situation or the patient.

Langs believes there is a need to define a correct, as compared to an incorrect, intervention. He says, "There is always a continuum and a gray area in the middle, but I find that the patient's unconscious responses to an intervention are a reliable guide. I don't agree with those analysts who think any one of five interventions can be made at a particular moment. I believe there is an optimal intervention and a correct moment or two for it to be given."

He refers to a quote of Winnicott's in 1971 in *Playing and Reality*: "It appalls me to think how much deep change I have prevented or delayed in patients in a certain classification category by my personal need to interpret. . . . If only we can wait, the patient arrives at understanding creatively and with immense joy, and I now enjoy this joy more than I used to enjoy the sense of having been clever."

8. There must be a one-to-one relationship with total privacy and confidentiality. This relationship expresses the ther-

apist's momentary "near-exclusive commitment" to the cure
of the patient's neurosis. This single-minded, single-rela-
tionship "therapeutic devotion" creates a maximum sense
of trust and the best possible opportunity for the patient
to express the neurosis and its underlying structure.

9. There must be an absence of any prior, concomitant or
posttreatment relationship between patient and therapist,
and the essential absence of physical contact. This safe-
guards the therapy and the relationship, as well as the patient's chances to get well.

10. The rule of abstinence must be carried out — extrathera-
peutic satisfactions between patient and therapist should
be avoided, including sexual and all other contacts, such
as meeting to discuss literary collaborations or attending
the same dinner party.

Langs calls these ground rules "a set of conditions that promise, to the greatest degree possible, neither to support nor gratify
the patient's emotional disturbance, consciously or unconsciously,
and to afford both patient and therapist a maximal degree of non-
pathological gratification in the absence of satisfactions of pathological needs and defenses." He adds, "Perhaps most crucial here
is the manner in which these conditions permit and encourage freedom of communication in the context of a specifically healthy mode
of relatedness — the ideal therapeutic symbiosis." The word "symbiosis" is used to describe the close relationship between mother and
infant before the latter starts to achieve a sense of self as separate
from the mother.

In dialogues with Dr. Leo Stone, an internationally famous psychoanalyst who lives in New York, which appeared as the book *The
Therapeutic Experience and Its Setting,* Langs declared that as he
re-examined the analogy between the mother-and-child relationship
and that of the patient and the analyst, it broke down at some point.
He found important differences, he said, in that the containment
the analyst offers the patient, unlike that of the mother, possesses
special deprivations designed to foster "suitable regression." This
enables the patient "to express his madness mainly on its own terms
rather than those of the therapist and to become analyzable, to generate the analytic material."

He explained further: "This means communicating and experiencing on some level very primitive inner perceptions, fantasies, anxieties and conflicts. This is not a characteristic of the maternal hold. The maternal hold fosters security and growth, without regression, and that's where the other elements in the analytic situation come in as crucial to what makes analysis distinctive and viable."

To which Stone had added, in the dialogue, "It's a unique human relationship, no doubt about it. It's a fact that Freud discovered more than even he knew."

When the ground rules are secure, Langs points out, the patient is able to accept "positive introjections" that strengthen the ego rather than "negative introjections" which provoke anger and fear. Introjection is the psychological process by which we identify with the analyst as we once did with our mother and father in childhood — one of the unconscious processes of learning.

The therapist's general manner (whether an accepting one, or, at times, because the therapist too is human, imbued with depression, irritability or anger) is important in that the patient accepts the therapist as model, part of cure. The management of the ground rules has the same implications, Langs says. Appropriate management and rectification, if needed, can lead to positive introjection — the constructive image of the therapist as taken in psychologically by the patient — and then insight. Whereas mismanagements "evoke negative introjects and uninsightful interludes."

Langs tells beginning therapists, "Any time you break a ground rule you have to resolve some issue within yourself. These rules are of a most delicate nature. If you modify them in the least, it's like giving up on therapy. We all instinctively go toward deviation, one of our defenses. But don't tolerate a deviant impulse. Don't rationalize it. Any time you catch yourself deviating, renounce it and analyze it. You'll pay for it if you give in to temptation. And so will the patient. Though sometimes a patient has to clobber you again and again, not only through encoded messages but directly, before you realize how much your deviation is affecting the therapy. When you correct it, you'll realize how much it has made you suffer a loss of immediacy, a loss of power."

He adds, "No matter how slight the deviation, it becomes a wedge in the relationship. The patient sees you as a greedy, devouring creature. His mother may have seemed to him like that when he was an infant — the interpretation of most therapists — but recognition of a deviation will quickly show that you *are* greedy and devouring, that this is not only a fantasy from the patient's past."

Langs believes that there are two basic therapeutic modalities: "It's either analytic or non-analytic. It's insightful or supportive. It's secure frame therapy or deviant frame therapy." In secure frame therapy the treatment unfolds around the patient's past traumas, there is basic trust of the therapist, and the anxiety created by constructive ground rules, such as a feeling of entrapment (every patient feels entrapped to some degree), becomes part of the normal treatment experience. In deviant frame therapy, there exists basic mistrust, pathological defenses, pathological forms of merger, plus the basic anxiety. There is also the satisfying of pathological instinctive drives.

A considerable measure of renunciation is required of both patient and therapist to bring about and keep a secure therapeutic setting and relationship. The natural wish in patient and therapist is for the immediate relief of tension and satisfaction of a desire. "Even in therapy," Langs says, "the detour necessary for mastery through understanding does not appear inherently attractive to either participant."

Therapists who refrain from making deviations are therapists capable of establishing and maintaining ultimate trust within their patients. They will also give sound interpretations based on the patients' reactions to them and to the past. Whereas therapists who deviate repeatedly lean toward noninterpretive interventions and make frequent errors in the interpretation of the patients' present and past, Langs says.

Other ground rules have developed over the years including the following:

1. There should be no touching except the shaking of hands at the start and end of therapy. If there is physical contact accidentally, such as patient and therapist bumping into each other, which produces an intense effect on the patient both erotically and aggressively, this should be analyzed.

2. The therapist should not accept phone calls during a patient's hour because the unconscious input in the patient will be negative.

3. The therapist should not start a session late or extend the hour beyond the time allotted.

4. There should be no knitting or any activity that keeps the therapist's hands busy, no matter what the rationalization ("I can think more freely").

5. There should be no eating or drinking by the therapist.

6. There should be no personal photographs of the therapist or the therapist's family in the office.

7. There should be no dogs or other pets in the room for they are inappropriate; they symbolize a member of the family or a family possession, a rival the therapist needs and loves, evoking anger in the patient.

8. The office should be in a professional building with a private waiting room, a bathroom, an entrance and a separate exit so there is no contact between patients.

9. There should be no exchange of gifts.

Langs comments on the last rule: "To give or accept a gift is a shared corruption. It is also a shared defense which usually includes a denial of rage, a denial of an appropriate degree of separatedness and a denial of the appropriate therapeutic relationship, including the agreed-upon fee. The fee should take care of all grateful feelings and if it does not, they should be analyzed, not acted out."

Langs describes the accepted gift (either on the part of therapist or patient) as "an attempt to form a pathological narcissistic misalliance and union, usually with a mother figure, or a symbolic attempt to live out pregnancy fantasies [the gift stands for the baby], rather than resolving the related separation anxieties." He says the gift undermines the basic model and climate of therapy "which should be an endeavor to move toward insight, verbalization, inner change, and ego maturation. It is a regressive gratification in mutual acting out; one can hardly expect the patient afterwards to attempt the far more difficult tasks of delaying gratification of needs and facing himself. Lastly, since such problems are always related to the patient's symptoms, resolution of these is unlikely or impossible under such conditions. The meanings of the gift must be explored and analyzed in terms of the patient's derivative associations. These derivatives will show that a gift should never be accepted by either therapist or patient."

There must be no tape recording of sessions, Langs says: "Taping is like note-taking. The therapist is bringing in a spy, a third party, an insulting deviation. The therapist has guaranteed his patient total privacy, total confidentiality. If he uses a tape recorder, the privacy and confidentiality is destroyed and this will be the adaptive context from then on. The patient will not easily forgive the therapist even after the deviation is rectified, if it is."

One therapist told a patient, "I'm tape recording this session. I won't play the tape for anyone. It's just for my files."

Langs comments, "This therapist is giving the patient a mixed message, the kind that always serves to make us feel a little crazy. He is saying he will not play the tape but obviously it will be in his files for anyone to hear, either with his permission or if the tape is stolen. This is an example of what I call madness in a therapist. Madness means giving all kinds of contradictory messages. It is mad for a therapist to say, 'You're guaranteed confidentiality but I think I'll tape you today'. That is what I call 'slanting', focusing on one message in order to obliterate other messages and meanings."

Langs feels strongly about the complex issues involved in insurance. He says, "What with insurance carriers having such a large place in treatment and the necessary reports by therapists, with malpractice suits as prevalent as they are, and with peer review procedures by therapeutic associations, it seems close to impossible to guarantee confidentiality to the patient, as well as to practice psychoanalysis. The ideal would be to have no insurance so that patients are fully responsible for treatment and there are no third parties. On the other hand, if insurance is absolutely necessary for a treatment, it must be maintained as an adaptive context, for the patient will work it over throughout treatment. We have to recognize that insurance provides pathological satisfactions and defenses and if a therapist misses this error, it will undermine treatment, even though it is carried on to a certain degree."

With Langs' own patients, and in supervision, his consistent approach is to inform the patient the treatment will be totally private and confidential. Should the patient introduce insurance, Langs explains this will have to be explored. Once the patient starts talking, the free associations show, without exception, Langs says, how destructive insurance is: "Patients then have a choice, either to stop insurance or to end the possibility of comprehensive truth therapy."

He referred to a paper by Dr. Gene Halpert in 1972 on the influence of insurance on analysis, which a number of Washington, D.C., analysts "tried to dispute." Langs reports, "Halpert had two patients who were covered one hundred percent by insurance and he found the analytic work paralyzed. There were no derivatives that could be interpreted. The patients had control of the situation, they were omnipotent. But when the insurance lapsed, he found an entirely different communicative field. So much depends on realizing how crucially the ground rules determine the communicative relationship."

Another ground rule which exists to protect the patient is that therapists should never discuss a patient by name among themselves, let alone in front of someone not in the profession, who might know the patient. A break in this ground rule has been known to occur, even among psychoanalysts, Langs says.

While it is the nonanalytic therapist who tends to deviate the most destructively, some analysts also break ground rules, according to reports of patients who have been in analysis with graduates of the New York Psychoanalytic Institute, the oldest, most renowned analytic institute in America, or with analysts from other institutes accredited by the American Psychoanalytic Association. There were such deviations as:

1. "My analyst ate supper during my 6 P.M. hour, four times a week. As the maid knocked on the door and brought in a tray, my analyst would tell me she did not have any other time to eat because she was going to an opera or a play the minute my hour ended."
2. "My analyst forgot my appointment twice in two years, making another appointment with someone who came from

out of town. When I appeared in the waiting room for my regular hour, he apologized, asked me to forgive him and said he would make up the hour, which he did."

3. "My analyst always knit through my entire session, and when I objected she said apologetically that it made her relax, that doing something with her hands put her more in touch with her thoughts about what I was saying."

4. "My analyst told me her husband was very ill and then later reported to me he had died, which made me feel very sorry for her."

5. "My analyst accused me of being very promiscuous; he said I would sleep with any man who came along and that I should be more selective."

6. "My analyst let me run six months behind in payments, because I was broke. Then I stopped going until I could pay what I owed. He wrote during this period that he missed me and hoped to see me soon but I never went back. I did however pay him what I owed."

7. "My analyst charged for a session I knew she had cancelled for I kept track of all sessions. But I could not convince her of this so I paid for a session I never had and always felt furious about it."

8. "My analyst, after I had described a number of times how my father had affairs, cheating on my mother, said one day, 'Your father was a real bastard'. I felt immediate shock. And my thought was, 'If she thinks my father is a bastard and she has said I am much like him, what must she think of me'?"

9. "My analyst would clip his fingernails during my session. The sound of his clipping away would make me very angry but I never said anything."

One psychiatrist from the West coast had nine therapists during twelve years spent in three cities where he attended medical school, then studied psychiatry, then practiced. Of these nine therapists, all of whom were classically trained, he says, the first one, a resident who treated him during medical school, helped most ("the most inexperienced therapist adhered the most to the ground rules").

After becoming aware of Langs' theories, this psychiatrist realized some of the serious effects on him of the breaking of ground rules during his therapy. He comments, "If you consider all the neurotic and psychotic relationships — marital, social, institutional and employment — you realize that people put up with a lot in order to survive, but you should not have to as a patient, where you expect the therapist to be at least neutral. And yet patients tolerate dreadful therapy — it's amazing what they suffer in the name of wanting to get acceptance and approval."

Among the breaking of ground rules he experienced in his twelve years of therapy were: the analyst talked with his (the patient's) relatives and, without permission, called his former analyst to get information about him; the analyst accepted insurance for much of the treatment but this was never discussed in depth; when, as a candidate in training, he asked about the timing of interpretations to patients, the therapist told him, "Well, it's like having a bowel movement — you just feel it coming on"; the analyst fell asleep repeatedly, then apologized on waking, explaining, "I'm not as young as I used to be."

This psychiatrist resigned an assistant director's position on an inpatient unit in a private hospital after the director, a psychiatrist, lectured him "on how to lie and to pad notes in the charts of Medicare patients so that extended hospital stays could be 'justified'." The director said there is " 'really big money in Medicare if you play the system the right way'."

I asked Langs during one interview, "Why is it a deviation to be five minutes late in seeing a patient?"

He answered, "Such a therapist is not taking his sessions seriously. He is setting a model of irresponsibility that will undermine the therapy. The patient will feel rage, hurt, rejection, loss of closeness, and defend against these feelings by denying them, displacing them and acting them out."

He illustrated what he meant. "One therapist was always late for the appointment of a forty-year-old woman. This was a woman who had never stolen a thing in her life. Yet now she found herself unaccountably stealing candy bars from drug stores. She felt the therapist had 'stolen' precious minutes from her and was unconsciously both copying him and acting out her wish for revenge in stealing 'sweets'."

I asked, "What about when patients are late or miss sessions?" I thought how I had been just the opposite, obsessively early and vowing never to miss a session unless mugged on the way uptown and left for dead in the angry streets.

Langs said, "The patient's responsibility for coming on time, or sessions missed because of illness, are perennially debated issues among therapists. The debate is endless because on a conscious level patients respond one way or another as to whether they are charged for a missed session but on an unconscious level they respond uniformly, virtually without exception. This latter response indicates to therapists that patients must always be held responsible for a missed session. The therapist should deal with the question of the absence on two levels: the reality of the cause for the absence and the dynamic aspects related to the conscious and unconscious perceptions, fantasies, conflicts, past experiences and meanings for the patient."

I asked, "When a patient is regularly late, doesn't the therapist consider this a major resistance?"

Langs said, "Often the patient's tardiness is a response to some deviation of the therapist. The therapist should recognize his input to the patient's lateness, rectify his error and interpret the patient's resistance accordingly."

He suggests therapists refrain from phoning patients when they fail to appear several times in a row. He says, "No attempt should be made to cajole, threaten or seduce the patient into continuing his therapy. This decision should remain the privilege and right of the patient. The therapist's role is to understand and interpret the conscious and especially the unconscious perceptions, fantasies and reasons on which the absence is based."

He mentioned a single man in his twenties who was depressed and struggling not to return to active homosexuality, as he had in the past when depressed. He had been in treatment with a therapist who charged for missed hours, and there were many because of the patient's business responsibilities. He had terminated treatment, he said, because he felt it unfair to be charged when he had to be absent on business.

In his initial interview with a new therapist, he said he would begin treatment only if he were not charged for sessions he had to cancel because of business. The therapist, wanting to provide much-needed therapy for this conflicted young man, agreed to his demand.

During the first few months of therapy, the patient attended every session. But after the therapist returned from vacation, the patient said he had to cover for vacationing office personnel and began to miss sessions. Occasionally he overslept for his 8 A.M. hour.

In a session that followed a cancellation, he spoke of the deaths of two friends and his fear of being old and alone. He expressed thoughts of traveling to South America with a male friend. He spoke of functioning well when forced to take responsibilities at work but said that when his mother let him sleep in the morning, he would miss half a day at work. He also mentioned he was afraid of getting close to people because they might detect his homosexuality.

Langs interpreted these associations as revealing some of the unconscious meanings of the deviant ground rules set for this patient: "His sanctioned absence was a means of combating his separation anxieties through denial of need and a repetition of the infantilization and seduction the patient experienced from his mother. Primarily his absence was a defense against latent homosexual perceptions of the therapist, based on the therapist's overly gratifying permission to miss scheduled hours. The acting out by the patient was in response to the error of the therapist."

I asked Langs, "Do therapists still hold to Freud's ground rule that during therapy no major decisions be made by the patient, that everything should be analyzed?"

He replied, "A major cause of acting out by patients is the acting out of therapists in forms not yet recognized. Sometimes when a therapist deviates, the patient will unconsciously move toward a major life decision, acting out his unconscious perceptions of the therapist. Since a therapist's deviations, or errors, are acts directed against the patient's therapeutic needs — against the patient — this may lead to acts by the patient as a form of unconscious sanction of the error or of revenge.

"The secure frame, which promotes working through, tends to diminish those forms of acting out that undermine the constructive aspects of treatment. At critical moments in the patient's life,

he is implicitly encouraged to explore, analyze and ultimately resolve, rather than to live out, as he might otherwise thoughtlessly
do. In withholding action, the conscious and unconscious meanings
of the particular situation, including the underlying perceptions, fantasies and conflicts, are likely to surface and he will be in a more
strategic position from which to resolve problems and achieve inner change."

Langs gives four "cautions" that, he says, are essential in expli-
cating the ground rule relating to major decisions by patients:

1. The patient's autonomy, his right to make his own decisions,
   and the vital necessity that he learn to do so, must be accepted and protected by the therapist. The latter should not
   use the exploration of major decisions to direct or guide the
   patient into a particular path or control him in any way—
   the patient should find his own way. Attempting to manipulate a patient is a common pitfall, one bound to be destructive since it deprives him of his relative independence. If
   therapists do not wish to infantilize their patients or use
   them to gratify their own narcissistic needs, they must never
   make important life decisions for them. To do so promotes
   helplessness, dependency and feelings of being used, and
   involves a kind of seductiveness that can only undermine
   insight psychotherapy. Making such a decision for a patient
   creates a situation where the therapist, on the one hand, is
   vulnerable to the patient's well-deserved rage should the decision he imposes be a poor one, and on the other hand,
   makes the patient unrealistically indebted to him if the decision works out.
2. Certain kinds of nondestructive acting out have adaptive
   and constructively experimental aspects. The therapist must
   not encroach upon the patient's right to, and need for, such
   behavior; he must interpret its pathological dimensions and
   leave the rest to the patient. There is a delicate balance here
   between interpretation and appropriate license, and the therapist should in general permit the patient as much freedom
   and lack of encroachment as feasible without entailing the

risks of behavior that will endanger the patient, others, or the therapy.

3. Such actions are to be viewed as meaningful communications and should be understood to contain valid, unconscious perceptions of the therapist and the meanings of the therapist's interventions and errors, especially the breaking of the frame. The implications of these actions, often grandiose, seductive or destructive, are to be understood and eventually integrated into the patient's understanding of himself.

4. Some patients may abuse this rule, as they misuse or use for resistance any of the ground rules, by delaying critical life decisions beyond all reasonable time for exploration in therapy. This too must be detected, explored and interpreted. Failing to act or decide is itself a decision, often a form of passive behavior that hides aggression, plus resistance, directed at the therapist and others.

Langs believes all resistances are interactional—there is a contribution from the patient in relation to the patient's pathological needs and a contribution from the therapist and what may be the therapist's unconscious needs. If the patient's resistances are frequent, the therapist should recognize they may be a result of mistrust on the part of the patient. A patient's silence is often response to a basic mistrust of the deviant therapist, Langs says. Silence may also serve as gratification of a defense but, as a rule, the adaptive context lies at the root of silence, in Langs' opinion.

Since silences are often both a major resistance and nonverbal form of expression, they should be interpreted as early in treatment as possible, Langs advises. If they are frequent, the therapist should listen to what the patient eventually says, bearing the silences in mind, and then try to interpret their meanings and uses.

Findings from the communicative approach show there are two forms of therapist silence, Langs says. One is the appropriate "holding, containing and waiting" when the patient's material does not permit intervention, either interpretation or the management of a ground rule. The other form of silence is a missed intervention, to which the patient will react negatively with derivative images of people who fail him, who don't understand him. The therapist must distinguish between these two forms of silence because inappropriate silence on his part promotes both inappropriate silence in the patient and acting out, Langs believes.

One patient, after the therapist had been silent for a full session, said sarcastically, "Are you dead?" Langs said that during supervision of this therapist it became clear he had an opportunity for interpretation but failed to intervene. The patient's response was the conscious comment that the therapist had died, which contained the unconscious perception of his having missed an intervention. Secondarily, the patient's remark reflected hostility because the therapist had not spoken.

Even if a therapist does something harmful to a patient, this may in certain instances be a stimulus for growth in two ways, Langs says. One is through paradoxical reactions to errors; the second is when the therapist recognizes his error, corrects it and interprets the patient's derivative responses that led to the correction.

"The question I have labored with a long time, and I don't have the full answer, is, 'Would the same or more effective growth occur without the damaging element'?" Langs muses. "I think there is probably some residual of hurt under conditions that hold therapists' errors. And that, at the very least, we should strive to help our patients grow to the greatest extent they can, without these negative inputs. We will never entirely eliminate them. I believe deliberate errors are more detrimental than inadvertent mistakes."

The patient will experience a different reality needed to face the traumatic past only when the therapist does not break ground rules, according to Langs. These rules are not arbitrary regulations set by Langs but have developed over the decades. Patients have made it clear they want to be "contained," respected, not taken advantage of emotionally—all qualities they felt lacking in the relationship between themselves as a child and their parents. When a ground rule is broken, patients are catapulted back into the trauma of childhood and they feel the therapists are no better than their parents or themselves and cannot help them.

Langs' students in the psychotherapy training program at the Lenox Hill Hospital, who are also members of the International Society for Psychoanalytic Psychotherapy, sometimes use humor as a way of highlighting Langs' teachings. The following was recently submitted to the Society's *Newsletter*:

TRUE CONFESSIONS OF A FRAMEWORK DEVIATOR

All right, I admit it, I was a framework deviator.

It started like all crimes, you know, petty nickel and dime jobs. I'd let a session run a few minutes over, or schedule an extra session here or there. Yeah, I accepted insurance, and no, I didn't charge for missed sessions. But hey, since I was seeing them at home it was really no sweat off my back. I'm sure you know how it goes, one thing led to another. I mean, how could I risk hurting their feelings by turning down some of the great gifts they brought me? Well, you guessed it, it all started getting a little out of hand. The more I deviated, the more they wanted to deviate.

Something had to be done. I was finally sent to the Robert Langs Reform School for Wayward Shrinks. We studied his Bibles and listened to his sermons. Every Friday was confession . . . "Forgive me, father, for I have sinned." He admonished us to return to therapy, to resolve our own madness. So, back I went. Working in the profession it wasn't easy to find a therapist I didn't already know. At last, I found an analyst. I told him of my sins and my guilt. If I wasn't sinning with my patients, I was burdening them with my guilt. There was always the introjected third party of Big Brother Bob watching my every move.

Well, my shrink gratified me with extra time, insurance, and he rarely charged for missed sessions. He spoke at length about the sins of my terrible mother and my harsh superego.

"Frame?" he asked. "Why's that such a big deal?" He said I must be crazy and offered medication.

I wonder how long it will be before I'm found sitting calmly in my padded cell, finally feeling contained. I quietly ponder Big Bob's book, *Madness in Psychotherapy,* to appear sometime in the future.

Another Society member wrote, under the title, "New Diagnostic Category for the DSM-IV" (*Diagnostic and Statistical Manual of Mental Disorders* of the American Psychiatric Association, whose third edition came out in 1980 and whose fourth is now being prepared):

> We have recently noted a new and highly contagious communicable disease: THE THIRD PARTY SYNDROME. This disorder becomes most readily apparent in those clinicians typified as Langsian psychotherapists. Symptomatology is likely to include: (1) Phobic avoidance of signing any forms including tax returns and pay checks. (2) Obsessive interpretation around vague third party derivatives as pertaining to insurance even when the patient is actually discussing his wife who recently called the therapist for a progress report. (3) Elements of depression stemming from efforts to integrate economic need vs. therapeutic benefit. Often these psychotherapists find themselves unable to resist the intense pressures to cooperate with their patients' seemingly incessant requests for insurance reimbursement.
>
> This syndrome might best be controlled through intensified supervisory contact. Such supervision in the Langsian mode must attend to at least portions of the therapist's pathology. The therapist/supervisor must help the psychotherapist metabolize the patients' introjected need for insurance. We therefore recommend that such essential and therapeutic supervision of this highly communicable disease qualifies for third party reimbursement.

Jest or not, Langs' adherents accept the importance of faithfully keeping the ground rules. They believe if any one rule goes by the board, so, for the moment, does therapy.

The therapist may make valid interpretations but the patient will not hear. For he remains unconsciously enraged by the breaking of the secure frame he needs as he embarks on the most courageous journey of all—the voyage into the inner self.

5
WHAT IS "CURE"?

One of the most challenging questions in therapy is "What is 'cure'?" The articles of psychoanalysts and other therapists are filled with references to "curing" patients, "easing mental pain," "doing away with symptoms" and "changing attitudes, characteristics and personality." Or most recently, "achieving a sense of self" and "increasing self-esteem."

What is the definition of cure? What should a patient expect of therapy? Will he change from a Mr. Hyde to a Dr. Jekyll? Will a female change from a Lucretia Borgia to a Florence Nightingale?

Will cure bring love? Will cure make us into a happy human being?

Psychoanalytic articles describe degrees of cure on the basis of the analyst's evaluation of changes that have taken place in the patient, such as, "His ego is strengthened, he is no longer controlled so strongly by his superego or id impulses." Patients have answered questionnaires as to why they believe they were cured, replying they feel less depressed, less driven, sexually freer, able to work more productively, less dependent on others, and not so selfish.

Dr. Walter A. Stewart, author of *Psychoanalysis: The First Ten Years* and *The Secret of Dreams,* former treasurer of the New York Psychoanalytic Institute, in delivering the A. A. Brill Lecture of 1980, declared, "Perhaps only now, having absorbed the impact of the fundamental discoveries of psychoanalysis are we in a position to move toward the building of a clinical theory that is based on the therapeutic experience that takes place between analyst-person and patient-person."

He continued: "*This* is still a large order. Neither we nor the patient can be certain what in the analytic process brings about a good therapeutic result. It is impossible to evaluate how much of that result is due to the patient's identification, not simply with the analyst, but with the analyst's *function* as analyst."

He quotes Dr. Kenneth Kenniston as suggesting that the most important aspects of analysis may be the analyst's "almost limitless respect for the individual, faith that understanding is better than illusion, insistence that our psyches harbor darker secrets than we care to confess, refusal to promise too much, and a sense of the complexity, tragedy and wonder of human life."

Dr. Stewart adds, "The identification of the patient with the analyst's analyzing function, which is part of the positive transference, is a blind spot in our analytic work, an unanalyzable given. It is impossible to measure the role of this important factor in the scientific understanding of the therapeutic process."

Dr. Stewart's thought that the patient must identify with the analyst's "function as analyst" intrigued me. It meant in part, for me, that the patient gains some understanding of the awesome power of the unconscious part of his mind and how it has influenced his life. The unconscious desires and thoughts are so intense that we spend much of our time denying them. They are too tormenting, too terrifying, too fearful to acknowledge. Jealousy so intense we wish to kill. Greed so devouring we would sell our souls to attain our desires. Sensual passion in childhood for forbidden people, such as parents and brothers and sisters.

I asked Langs what he meant by that amorphous, intangible quality of inner change called "cure" and how it was achieved. He replied, "I think of cure as a visionary goal that permits the patient to feel more at ease with himself and others. It occurs not through intellectual insight but through the automatic, unconscious processes by which we become in large part what we are from infancy on."

Among these processes, he said, is the emotional taking-in from the therapist anything he does that conveys his feelings, as we originally did from our parents through their words, attitudes, acts, facial expressions, unconscious wishes, conscious wishes. This is the *only* way we change — through sensing feelings in others and ourselves. How the therapist feels towards the patient — hostile or caring, loving or hating, unconsciously wishing to help or destroy — is the way the patient will feel about himself.

Langs gave me his article "Modes of 'Cure' in Psychoanalysis and Psychoanalytic Psychotherapy," which had appeared in 1981 in the *International Journal of Psycho-Analysis*. Because it is an important article and some of his concepts are in terms that cannot easily be translated into popular language, meant only for the eyes of psychoanalysts, I will quote indirectly from it for the most part.

He starts off saying there are no "definitive studies" describing "cure" and he will attempt "to clarify selected aspects" of the problem of defining cure.

He describes three "modes of cure," each with its characteristic forms of "listening, formulating, intervening, relating and alleviating symptoms and vulnerability to remission."

He defines these three modes briefly as: (1) work with the manifest material (the direct words of the patient; (2) work with the isolated intrapsychic derivatives (the words of the patient interpreted on an unconscious level as related to his past); and (3) work with derivatives that are understood within the context of the ongoing unconscious communicative interaction of patient and therapist.

He says that current therapeutic and analytic practice, as reflected in the literature, is concentrated almost entirely on the first two of these modalities and there has been insufficient recognition and use of the third and most comprehensive mode of cure.

He does not distinguish between psychoanalysis and psychoanalytic psychotherapy because, he says, their "differences are negligible in the areas I will address." Since the material to illustrate psychoanalysis was more readily available, he explains, most of his examples are drawn from the analytic situation. He uses the term neurosis in its broadest sense, taking in psychoses and the narcissistic, psychosomatic and character disorders.

He notes a wide discrepancy between the psychoanalytic concept of neurosis and prevalent therapeutic procedures. He points out that Freud's "remarkable realization of the critical role of unconscious fantasy constellations" responsible for neurotic behavior are represented in disguised form in the conscious free associations of the patient.

He mentions "pathological unconscious fantasy constellations" as the cause of neurosis and says they lead to the unveiling of psychic tension within a person and the conflicts Freud described. These fantasy constellations show the disruptive influences in the patients' early relationships with their mothers and fathers. What he calls "the neurotic syndrome" is "an attempt at adaptation which misfires, largely because of the overriding influence of a hierarchy of pathological unconscious fantasy constellations and perceptions."

This brief and oversimplified concept, Langs explains, forms the basis of what he describes as the three modes of cure: Types A, B and C. In discussing Type A — listening to the manifest or surface content of the patient's associations and making interpretations — he gives as example a vignette the late Dr. Ralph Greenson, prominant psychoanalyst who lived in Los Angeles, mentioned in a volume on psychoanalytic technique.

A female patient one morning told Greenson he looked "different," then quickly changed the subject to talk of trivia. Greenson pointed this out to her, suggesting she was "running away from something," that perhaps she had positive feelings for him. She became uncomfortable, and he asked why it was so difficult for her to tell him of these positive feelings. She said she was afraid of being laughed at.

Analysts characterize such efforts as "working with" or "analyzing" the transference, Langs explains. The efforts form the basis for interpretations on a surface level when material emerges regarding the analyst, and the interpretations are justified as "analysis of the transference."

He asks, "If, however, as seems generally agreed, neuroses are based on *unconscious* fantasy constellations and perceptions, how can such work have a curative effect? The literature abounds with claims of symptom alleviation based on such techniques, which clearly cannot be founded on true insight into *unconscious* processes and contents. Not only are listening, formulating and intervening carried out on a manifest level but also the essential analytic relationship is being addressed entirely on the surface. Unconscious communication from both patient and therapist are excluded from consciousness or denied, and a form of surface relatedness is developed."

The second mode of cure, Type B, work with isolated or what Langs calls "Type One" derivatives, is the analytic procedure that characterizes most writings on psychoanalytic technique, he says. Work with the manifest or surface content shades into efforts to approach what the patient is saying on an unconscious level, though these efforts are "ultimately misguided," Langs adds.

The analyst "infers" some unconscious process or content from the patient's conscious thoughts, behaviors and fantasies and "typically involves the patient's purported use of unconscious displacement, projection or denial." But introjective mechanisms — what the patient has unconsciously taken in from the therapist as stimuli for the patient's fantasies or behavior — are not considered.

Also, little attention is paid to the ground rules, their management and the interpretation of impingements. And virtually "no consideration is given the ongoing unconscious communicative interaction except at moments of acute crisis or direct allusion to the therapist or therapeutic situation. The therapist's interventions are understood almost entirely in terms of surface meaning and intention. The patient's unconscious perceptions of the therapist and the existence of a continuous introjective process on the patient's part are relatively unrecognized in his relationship with the therapist."

While work on the surface level is carried out with almost total denial of the analyst's countertransference, there is some acknowledgement of the possibility of "distorted inputs" on the analyst's part. But these inputs are viewed as quite rare and only when there is a gross therapeutic error. "During such interludes, much is made of the patient's *conscious* detection of these mistakes and his *conscious* reactions to them," Langs says. "Little attention is afforded his unconscious responses."

He gives another example cited by Greenson of a patient who was reluctant to tell him she was having sexual thoughts about him. She knew he was married and she believed he could not possibly care for her after all he had learned about her. Finally, with much embarrassment, she spoke of her fantasies, of Greenson holding her in his arms. She said while alone in bed she thought of him as her lover. Greenson asked her to describe what she would like to do sexually with him.

The patient said she wanted him to crush her in his arms to the point where she could hardly breathe, lift her off the floor and carry her to bed where they would "make love." Greenson asked what she meant by "making love." She described the image of his tearing off her nightgown, kissing her so hard on the lips she could barely breathe, forcing her legs apart and ramming his penis into her. She described his penis as huge and said it would hurt but she would love the feeling. She then mentioned an odd detail: his face was unshaven and his beard scratched her cheek.

Greenson viewed these fantasies as reflecting masochistic wishes and linked them to her attack of asthma at six, when her mother married the patient's sadistic stepfather. Greenson offered the interpretation that he was viewed as the sadistic stepfather gratifying the patient's masochistic, guilt-laden Oedipal wishes.

He then asked her to recall what man had scratched her with his beard when she was a little girl. She remembered that her stepfather would hurt her by squeezing her close so she could hardly catch her breath, then throwing her into the air. This gave validation, according to Greenson, of the basis of her fantasies about him as a lover.

Langs asserts, "Here the patient's conscious fantasies are understood as based on an unconscious displacement of experiences (and fantasies) involving her stepfather. Greenson suggests that an experience from the past has been taken over intact, displaced into the present, and experienced toward the analyst, due entirely to an intrapsychic need within the patient, with no contribution by the analyst. He is understood as creating a setting within which such experiences can take place. Projection and displacement prevail, and no consideration is given to the possibility that the analyst has intervened in some way that could have stimulated these fantasies or could perhaps even have formed a basis for valid unconscious perceptions of some similarity between the analyst and the patient's stepfather — that on some unconscious level, the analyst's communications have been aggressive, sexual or hurtful."

Langs says, in this scholarly article, that the psychoanalytic community has accepted this level of listening and intervening as offering "the optimal analytic experience, and as a basis for the insightful resolution of neuroses" but that he questions this type of analytic effort.

He then explains what he calls "Type Two" derivatives organized around the "adaptive context" within the therapeutic interaction. This is the process used by the analyst in the third mode of cure, Type C. Here every association and act by the patient "is analyzed in the light of the stimulus or *adaptive context* that has provoked it." Extensive evidence, he says, suggests these precipitants are "almost without exception the silences and interventions of the analyst."

In the third mode of cure, such silences and interventions are examined in depth in terms of what they communicate, both consciously and unconsciously, to the patient. They are seen "as part of the ongoing, spiralling conscious and (especially) unconscious communicative interaction that takes place between patient and therapist in both psychotherapy and psychoanalysis." All other stimuli, whether from within the patient or traumatic outside relationships, are seen as secondary adaptive contexts and are, as a rule, linked to a primary adaptive context within the therapeutic experience, Langs maintains.

He asks that important distinctions be made by the therapist between "the intrapsychically determined unconscious fantasies" and "the introjects based primarily on valid unconscious perceptions of the implications of the therapist's silences and interventions."

Both introjective and projective processes should be considered fully. In addition, the patient's derivative communications should be understood to contain both distorted and valid perceptions and responses.

Langs reiterates his challenge to therapists: "I have been repeatedly able to demonstrate the extensive pathological unconscious communications contained in the therapist's and analyst's erroneous interventions and mismanagement of the ground rules. With remarkable consistency, patients unconsciously perceive and introject the implications of these errors.

"Similarly, when an analyst intervenes properly, representations of a positive introject and Type Two derivative validation ensue, which serve to reorganize available material, thereby shedding new light on its implications. This type of psychoanalytic listening and intervening requires of the analyst considerable self-knowledge and a consistent monitoring of the conscious and unconscious implications of his silences and interventions."

The therapist who does not take into account his own unconscious thinking and its possible effect on the patient's free associations and behavior may profess to be helpful and to seek out the "truth" but unconsciously "his need is to exclude its most pertinent representations," in Langs' words. Such a therapist undermines the patient's capacities to know reality. The therapist dreads his own unconscious fantasies, as well as those of the patient. The patient perceives this fear and tries to deal with it "if in no other way than by sealing it off behind the barrier system in collusion with the therapist."

Sometimes the unconscious realization within the patient of the psychopathology and anxieties of the therapist "generates a relatively positive self-image within the patient, to the point that some degree of symptomatic relief may ensue," Langs adds. This relates to the patient's unconscious awareness "that the therapist is not God, that he too has conflicts he cannot resolve."

In his concluding comments, Langs states: "The present paper presents a clear challenge to current psychoanalytic practice. It asks that responses be based on sound psychoanalytic methodology and the use of a sophisticated validating process in which indirect, Type Two derivative validation is a central criterion.

"On this basis it should prove feasible for each individual analyst to re-evaluate his technique and to make, if this is indicated, the necessary adjustments suggested here. My own view of the technical consequences of the concepts presented here is that they require only a few—though essential—revisions in listening and intervening. The net effect, however, would be considerable."

Present techniques only serve to afford both patient and therapist "a means of unconscious pathological merger and of obtaining pathological symbiotic gratifications," Langs says. Should the alleviation of symptoms occur, it is based in part on the "consequent setting aside of separation anxieties and of the sense of separateness between patient and therapist." But the process of achieving a sense of identity is impaired for the patient.

In contrast, the use of Type Two derivative interpretations and the securing and maintenance of the ground rules offer the patient a holding form of relatedness that reflects "a healthy pattern of symbiosis that is growth-promoting, and fosters autonomous functioning in both participants."

In this paper, Langs' theories were described for the first time to an international audience. He had a readership that consisted of the classical psychoanalysts of the world. He realized, he told me, this would be a very resistant audience, made up of analysts trained in the "defensive" clinical approach set by Freud.

Langs said he thought that a young therapist in the psychotherapy training program at Lenox Hill Hospital had an easier time accepting the idea of an interactional role with the patient than the experienced therapist who "believes he is well analyzed when he is not. He has maintained his defenses within the system designed to protect these defenses. It is catastrophic for him to give up the defenses he has used automatically to protect against the truth."

Such a therapist, Langs adds, "will say that the patient is going to experience him as hostile no matter what he says or does because that is the way the patient perceives his parents. But this is one of the analytic myths. When it comes to unconscious perception, the patient functions well. We are not sick unconsciously. It is our conscious mind that makes us sick. A patient would not perceive the therapist as hostile if he were not actually hostile in some way."

The interactional approach assumes there is a "lot more health in patients" rather than assuming the patient is sick and denying the validity of any perception by the patient that the analyst may be acting out of unhealthy, unrecognized wishes or acts.

"The healthy therapist brings out the best functioning in the patient on an unconscious level," Langs says. "He accepts and deals with the patient's valid perception of him. If he is unaware the patient is telling him some truths about himself, he cannot help the patient. Change in the patient takes place when the truths he is telling the therapist about the therapist are accepted."

Langs was saying, I gathered, that only as the patient senses the therapist is honest with himself can the patient then try to be honest with *himself*. The ability to face the self squarely is a rare one, given the strength of resistances, but therapists are expected to be able to do this to a greater degree than patients. Langs' message is that they should work even harder at knowing themselves if they expect to cure patients.

The need to be cured and to cure is a basic need Langs says exists in everyone in relation to human experiences. Among other needs are: for boundaries or ground rules; for relatedness; to communicate; to express instinctual drives; to erect defenses against terrifying, maddening feelings and fantasies and the need for a cohesive self, a sense of identity. There may be others to discover, he adds: "I learn by keeping an open mind, alert to possible changes, to discoveries that lie ahead. I also learn by finding out I am wrong. Sometimes you have to try many ways before you can validate the correct response."

"Cure" also comes in part, Langs maintains, perhaps in large part, from the patient's identification with a healthier figure than the mother and father of childhood. If the therapist is not that healthier figure, the patient will not be analyzed but tend to act out what he senses as the unhealthy unconscious wishes of the therapist.

Langs cites, as illustration, the case of a female of twenty-eight in therapy with a male therapist twenty years older, who had never married. She fell romantically in love with this older therapist, whom she had been seeing four years. She told him of her wish to marry him after a dream in which she fantasied he made love to her. He interpreted the dream by saying, "That's the feeling you had as a little girl for your father."

A few months later she met an older man who was divorced and lived in a distant city. After a whirlwind courtship, he proposed and she decided to marry him. The therapist had been talking of terminating her therapy and she felt in a panic, knowing she still had many conflicts to face and solve. But she did not dare oppose the therapist's decision and his order, "Try standing on your own feet."

She sensed his wish to get rid of her, sensed also at times his seductive manner, implying an unconscious wish he could have married her — a young, attractive, financially successful woman. She carried out his wish to end the analysis as she moved, bag and baggage, from New York, where she gave up her job with a large advertising firm, to Los Angeles, where her husband practiced law. After only a few weeks as his wife, she discovered he was impotent.

She had, in a sense, married her therapist, replacing him with a like figure, a man who could not have sex with her. She was unconsciously telling her therapist not only that he was impotent sexually (or he would have married) but also that his interventions were impotent — he had not been an effective therapist. He had broken ground rules left and right, including ending the therapy arbitrarily, when termination should be a mutual undertaking.

Patients expect their therapists to have faced unconscious conflicts to a degree where they can be effective with patients, Langs is saying. If therapists are not conscious of hostile and seductive feelings aroused by patients but inflict them on patients unknowingly, the latter have no chance to identify with someone mentally healthier than they are, and remain doomed to depression, never knowing why. They may experience the temporary relief of some symptoms but they will not achieve that inner change which allows them to love and to work effectively, gives a greater ease to existence, and strengthens self esteem.

But what is the "self"?

We could say that before Freud discovered the overwhelming passions that whirled in the unconscious part of the mind, the "self" was what man consciously perceived. But, since Freud, any complete concept of the self takes in the unconscious mind too. When a patient starts analysis, he thinks of the self only as that part of him of which he is aware. Then — usually to his shock, horror and dismay — he learns there is another part of the self. It is a part he has used much of his precious energy to deny over the years. It is the most important part of himself, he finally, albeit reluctantly, admits.

Psychoanalysts discovered that our "self" develops over the years out of everything we have ever experienced and our unconscious fantasies and desires, as well as what we consciously feel about the self, such as esteem or confidence, or conversely, lack of self esteem or self confidence. There is the self we know and the self we do not know. The Bible said (Romans 7:15), "I do not do what I want, but I do the very thing I hate," implying unconscious motives. When Freud wrote, "Where there is id, let ego be," as the goal of analysis, he was saying that, as the unconscious becomes conscious, we have a chance to handle our conflicts, both those from the past that we have buried and the current ones.

Among the psychoanalysts who have studied the development of the self is Dr. Otto Kernberg. He delivered a paper, "Self, Ego, Affects, and Drives," at a panel on "Psychoanalytic Theories of the Self" presented at the Fall meeting in New York of the American Psychoanalytic Association in December, 1980. In this paper he declared that most psychoanalysts agree that "the gratifying, blissful states we knew as infants with our mothers constitute the core of the ego's self-feeling or self-experience." He added, "Some [psychoanalysts] would go so far as to consider the building up of an integrated concept of the self on the basis of such early merger experiences as constituting the final, integrated, normal self."

The development of the concept of the self also occurs "at times of heightened frustration and painful or traumatic experiences" that "will later evolve into frightening, aggressive, and devalued experiences of the self and into frightening, agressive, sadistic representations of objects [others]," he said. The concept of the development of the self "under both libidinal and aggressive conditions" is accepted today by many psychoanalysts, including himself, he added.

At the same panel, Dr. William Grossman, noted psychoanalyst, spoke on "The Self as Fantasy: Fantasy as Theory." He stated that the "self-state description" is, according to psychoanalytic theory, constructed in the same way as any mental product, that is, of feelings, impulses and ideas "in the form of a fantasy construction."

He explained: "In the case of the self-state, the language of this fantasy is everyday language about an everyday fantasy about a fantasized entity, 'the self.' The 'self' is the term popularly used to provide an organizational point of reference for inner experiences. It therefore seems to be a concrete entity, and is treated like an experiential 'fact.' The 'self,' then, is a special fantasy with its own language and referents. It is caught up in the popular discourse in the language of self-experience. It is anchored in and derives a sense of immediacy from the bodily experiences, activities, and emotional interactions with other people."

As a result of my analysis, I found my concept of "self" changing. For one thing, as I realized how I had unconsciously taken in attitudes, beliefs and actions identified with my mother and father (not to mention their fantasies and wishes), I agonized, "Who is really *me*?" I had to look at what I had unconsciously imitated in them in order to survive emotionally — who else was I to copy? I also felt less beset by my own strong emotions of love and hate as I could accept my parents as victims of their unhappy childhoods.

For another, as I could understand the losses of childhood that had gone unmourned, both the real and the fantasied losses, the growing acceptance of these losses which I had never faced, but which had taken a toll of my life, lessened depression and I felt a stronger sense of self.

I also felt less driven, I could tolerate empty hours, did not have to fill them with obsessive work or useless entertainment. And as my anger could be expressed at the analyst, I realized who were the early targets of my fury and rebellion — why should I hate a stranger? I became aware, as I could be more reflective, of how self destructive I often was. I faced the child in me who still wanted to be taken care of by my mother and father or a reasonable or unreasonable facsimile thereof. I understood too how much I wanted to be a boy, like my envied younger brother, helped along in this wish by my mother and father who had wanted their firstborn to be a son.

At first I resented the analyst's interpretations as criticism, wanting only his praise and love. But slowly I realized the pure psychic gold of an interpretation, how I could use it to advance a hair's breadth further into the knowledge of the unconscious self.

I had sought and remained in psychoanalysis for many years believing it would bring an end to life's torment. But, as the analyst informed me, psychoanalysis is not magic, it would not solve the problems life held that stemmed from reality. I found that as I could understand the inner self more, life's expected conflicts did not strike such terror into my heart.

Most important, I had to learn how to *listen* to the therapist. At first his interpretations, because of the pain they caused, were not really "heard." He had to repeat them, sometimes over and over and in different context, before I could "hear" them in the marrow of my bones, so to speak.

Listening to the inner self, really hearing and understanding the words you utter in analysis, is the new capacity you acquire when therapy is effective. It is a capacity you then are able to use when you are alone. You acquire the capacity only by becoming aware of how the analyst listens to you. As you understand how he listens and interprets what you have told him, you can listen in the same way to your inner self.

Langs is asking that this quality of being able to listen be even more finely attuned in the therapist so that therapy can be more effective.

6
THE DUMPING
DEFENSE

Peripheral to cure is a concept Langs often mentions—"projective identification." It interferes with cure and prevents cure from taking place, when indulged in by the wild therapist.

Langs simplifies the term by calling it "dumping." He says it is used as a defense against the recognition of inner feelings. For instance, the man next to you on a plane may suddenly start confiding the details of his unhappy life, how his wife does not understand him, his children are selfish little beasts, his mother-in-law is the prime witch of the world.

You may feel flattered at first because he has chosen to confide in you but then, after an hour of listening, you feel exploited and misused. And angry—both at yourself for allowing your time to be taken up, when you wanted to do your own work or perhaps just enjoy the pleasure of silence and reflection, and at the insensitivity of a person who dumps his woes on you instead of seeing a therapist.

Melanie Klein first described projective identification and its excessive use by schizophrenic patients as an unconscious defense that serves to get rid of inner tension. It allows them to express desires and fantasies and feelings that threaten their mental balance so overwhelmingly that their first concern is to project them onto someone else; they do not care on whom. They do not, however, have enough of a sense of psychic leisure to listen to anyone else's woes.

Some analysts do not believe projective identification is a useful concept. One said, "I think of it as a defense mechanism that exists in a person's mind and is unconscious. He projects his feelings on someone else who hears the surface message and reacts to it with his own defense mechanisms which are similar to or complement the other person's."

Langs explains: "Projective identification is a psychological defense we all use at times, whether in therapy or not. We experience it daily at the hands of those we love, or strangers, as they overwhelm us with aspects of their inner world, hurling at us their complaints, fantasies, daydreams, conflicts."

I asked, "How does it differ from identification?"

"The mental process of identification works in the opposite direction, as we 'take in' an attribute rather than project it upon someone else," he said. "Through identification in childhood with our mother and father we incorporate their traits — some constructive, some destructive — into the image of the self and ways of functioning."

"Is identification a beneficial process or a destructive one?"

"When not excessive, it can be beneficial. But excessive use of it leads to a loss of personal identity and inner turmoil, based on the contradictory elements of the identifications. For instance, if a mother is very disturbed, the child will identify with both her nondisturbed characteristics and the disturbed ones, and feel in conflict."

He calls projective identification "a rather strange term." He explains: "It implies that a given individual sends outward — extrudes — impulses and fantasies, or some disturbing aspect of his or her inner state. The term dumping captures this process because it implies the person attempts to place into someone else an aspect of his inner mental world. To do so, the target person must be present and there must be an interactional thrust."

He prefers the term "interactional projection," because projective identification implies the presence of another person and the reaction between the one who dumps and the one dumped into. Langs describes interactional projection as both a riddance mechanism and an interpersonal appeal for help in managing inner confusion by trying to get rid of it.

The most common purpose of dumping is to get rid of threatening inner conflicts, perceptions and fantasies by attempting to establish them in another person. The goal is to have this other person serve as receptacle for distasteful or dangerous thoughts and feelings and also to take in qualities from the other person that will relieve anxiety. Dr. Martin Wangh, internationally prominent psychoanalyst, calls this "the evocation of a proxy" because it is a plea for help.

Patients are expected to engage in dumping, therapists are not. But some therapists do, Langs says. He explains: "A therapist may use language primarily to get rid of personal pathology rather than for symbolic communication designed to impart insight. Instead of making a valid interpretation, the therapist discharges disturbing thoughts or fantasies into the patient. The therapist does not understand why the patient acts out, or why the analysis or therapy is not going well.

"Patients should expect a therapist to receive their 'dumped' thoughts and fantasies but a patient should not have to cope with the therapist dumping aspects of his problems into the patient. Here the therapist is trying to use the patient to cure himself."

Dumping is involved in all modifications of the basic conditions of treatment, each with a specific quality in keeping with the nature of the deviation, Langs says. An increase in fee "dumps the therapist's greed into the patient, while a reduction in fee offered in the face of a threat that a patient may terminate, dumps the therapist's own separation anxieties and overindulgent tendencies. Ruptures in confidentiality tend to dump highly aggressive forms of betrayal into the patient, who is then under some pressure interactionally to work over the extruded contents."

Langs calls projective identification a major factor in all "action-discharge" types of therapy. This includes therapies that urge patients to scream, to display violent feelings, to "confront" each other in group therapy, or to "decondition." Such therapies may give temporary relief by affording patients the chance to dump some of their pathological feelings into therapists who then give ineffective but responsive interpretations. Persons who have grown up with unresponsive parents are often willing to accept any kind of response with gratitude, Langs points out.

Many forms of psychotherapy are basically designed to foster the pathological dumping efforts of the therapist, he says. Since this wish primarily operates unconsciously in the therapist burdened with inner conflicts, that therapist will turn avidly to schools of psychotherapy that sanction the use of this type of pathological interactional and interpersonal mechanism, thus explaining their popularity. Langs says, "Often, the dumping tendencies of the therapists sanction similar propensities in the patient. There will be exchanges of projective identification between patient and therapist that become more and more violent and disruptive because neither participant to treatment is capable of containment and metabolizing."

Quite often, Langs adds, a patient who identifies closely with a therapist, will start to "dump" in outside relationships as well. Therapists who have an unconscious need to dump conflicts into patients approve of this, mistakenly viewing it as a sign of emotional health, the freedom to speak openly to others of inner burdens. This misunderstanding forms the basis for many corrupt and collusive treatments, Langs charges. He says he thinks one of the unconscious motives for becoming a therapist "is to make pathological, inappropriate use of the patient as a container for pathology."

In a distorted way, he says, patients at times gain momentary relief when they are able to successfully take in and "contain" the pathological projective identifications from therapists and experience them in a state of "reverie," a term used by Wilfred R. Bion, European psychoanalyst, for "containing" projective identifications. But as a rule patients become overwhelmed and the consequences, Langs says, are "rather destructive."

Bion called the projected contents the "contained" and referred to the recipient as the "container." In therapy the patient dumps aspects of his pathology into the therapist, and it is the therapist's responsibility to "contain" these contents and work or "metabolize" them into an understanding of the patient without the therapist feeling he is masochistic. The term "metabolize" was first used by Dr. Robert Fliess who noted in 1942 that analysts temporarily identify with the patient, "metabolize" that experience, and make an interpretation.

Langs explains, "We do this both cognitively [with intellectual awareness] and in the interactional sphere [relating consciously and unconsciously] to the patient. That's really the essence of the listening process. And we consistently sort out how much comes from the patient in projective identification and how much from ourselves."

He warns, "If the therapist doesn't become conscious of the nature of the patient's projective identification, he may then unconsciously reproject it. In 1962 Leo Grinberg, a European psychoanalyst, gave that process a name: projective counteridentification. It sounds rather complex but it means you dump back into the patient without understanding that you do, and the patient has even more of a burden to carry."

When a therapist, listening to a patient, feels a sense of oppression, or under pressure, or empty, he is undergoing "negative projective identification," in Langs' words. He should try to understand why the patient's projective identification is affecting him in this fashion in order to "metabolize" it into deeper understanding of the patient. Usually what the patient is saying touches off in the therapist some unresolved conflict of his own.

Patients will unconsciously convey their experiences of projective identification from the therapists in their free associations. One woman told her therapist that her mother was a forceful, probing woman who made unfounded comments, withheld information and made her feel attacked and confused. These thoughts confirmed a subjective impression that her therapist was "forcing" his conflicts into her, making her feel attacked and confused.

Therapists should become aware of projective identifications that stem from interactional pressures and determine how much of the projective identification stems from the patient and how much from the therapist, Langs says.

Anyone who has had to listen interminably to a friend's or relative's account of personal misery and fancied injustices knows the feeling of the "dumping" process. That it comes out of the speaker's inner anxiety does not make it a pleasurable experience for the listener. To hear of someone else's troubles is to remind yourself of your own and to become depressed. At least the therapist is paid to take the "dumping" and use it to help the patient face inner feelings.

One woman, realizing her friends were using her as a verbal garbage pail, felt overwhelmed and weary after hours of hearing complaints. Finally, fed up with a saga of sorrows, she said to the complainer, "Why don't you go to a therapist? Or else let me charge you for my time."

If too much is dumped into us too early in life by a mother or father, it may drive us mad. In like fashion, if a very emotionally disturbed person goes to a therapist who dumps many personal conflicts into the patient, it may drive the patient mad, and as he breaks down, he will attack the therapist in encoded form, an automatic defense against dealing with threatening problems head-on, Langs says. The fear of telling the therapist directly that he is crazy is too dangerous to the patient, who needs the therapist as ally, who is afraid of the therapist's power to destroy if questioned. But, giving an unconscious message, the patient may speak of "unseen enemies, gangsters, Nazis, Russian spies" out to destroy him.

Langs sees the breaking of a ground rule as an expression of "madness," an attempt by the therapist "to defend against his own madness." He believes, for instance, that the therapist who sees a patient in his home may say this does not affect treatment, that the patient's feelings about being in the therapist's home are freely expressed and may even contribute important material to the analysis. Langs believes this is rationalization, that usually therapists use their homes as offices to save money or to avoid daily fighting the traffic on their way to and from a separate office.

He says, "When the therapist brings a patient into his home, it is unconsciously both a hostile and seductive act. The patient will feel he is part of the personal life of the therapist who cannot separate the intimacy of home from professional work. The patient is close to the therapist's bedroom, dining room and kitchen from which odors emanate. Even if he never sees a member of the family, he may hear their voices and fantasize what they are like, and their very closeness is always with him.

"This setting creates a barrier that I think is impossible to overcome. The patient will sense the therapist as someone who cannot separate himself from his family, needs the protection of the home setting and fears to be alone with the patient. How can such a therapist help a patient separate himself from his parents or from the therapist? The latter is telling the patient, 'It's okay to merge with others, it's dangerous to be alone with someone you fear.' Such a therapist is unconsciously infantilizing the patient as the therapist wants to be infantilized, close to his family twenty-four hours a day. This is pathology but a lot of people live by pathological means. If you take it away, they believe they will die."

The patient essentially wants the complete privacy of a professional office, desires the "ideal containment, the proper amount of distance from the therapist's personal life, " Langs believes, and is harmed by the confused feelings aroused whenever he enters the therapist's home.

Langs calls it madness when a therapist dumps his feelings into a patient. In addition to unconscious dumping on patients, some therapist give "mixed messages," he says, stating one thing but conveying a second meaning. A therapist may also unconsciously act hostilely or seductively toward a patient, and if the patient responds with conscious or unconscious thoughts about his sexual or aggressive feelings toward the therapist, the latter may show anger as his unconscious defense against awareness of feelings. Langs also says a therapist may unconsciously use seductiveness to gain an outlet for hostile feelings or hostility as an outlet for sexual feelings.

One psychoanalyst in her seventies, who never had children, listened to a thirty-year-old patient recall that when she was coming out of the anesthetic at a hospital where she had an abortion, she was sobbing as though her heart would break and crying out, "Where is my baby? I want my baby."

The analyst said skeptically, "I don't believe you said that."

The patient, shocked at being called a liar, asked, "What do you mean?"

"You didn't say that," repeated the analyst.

"I remember saying it," the patient defended herself. "What's more my sister was sitting next to the bed as I gained consciousness. I asked her the next day if she had heard me say this and she said she did. That it had upset her because I was crying so hard."

The analyst was silent. She did not apologize or in any way explain her attack. After that the patient never felt free to say what she thought since she had been called a liar for telling the truth. This was more than a matter of name-calling. The therapist was dumping into the patient her own fears and guilts about not having borne a child, as well as showing her own difficulties with reality, and her mistrust of the patient — she was unable to give the patient a secure holding.

It is difficult, even for those in therapy, much less those who are not and never will be, to understand the primitive, unconscious part of the mind, reservoir for all our mad repressed fantasies. What we call "mad" in an adult is not the same as the primary process thinking of childhood before reason takes over. Though there are "mad" children who cannot control themselves or repress their feelings and thoughts so excessively that they become catatonic. When an adult commits murder, incest or rape or regresses to a psychotic state, we think of him as "mad," controlled not by the rational part of the mind but driven out of his wits by intense, distorted, crazy fantasies. Some have "mad" moments when they feel out of control, or fear they will lose control.

Anyone who wants to be a therapist, Langs says, has to face what he calls "the madness within all of us," otherwise the therapist cannot help patients face their madness. Langs maintains, "Not enough therapists in their training are helped to face madness and may do mad things with patients. Some act out of a benign madness, others are utterly mad and take out lustful and vengeful feelings on patients in an exploitative way."

Everything in therapy, Langs is saying, is an interactional process — even dumping.

7
COLLUSION
AGAINST
THE TRUTH

Too much is asked of therapy in that we expect magic from it. But not enough is asked in that the quality of therapy, outside of psychoanalysis, is not questioned enough by those who seek it.

Perhaps we should not be expected to behave more intelligently, or less neurotically, about selecting a therapist than a surgeon or a Congressman. A surgeon is involved in our physical survival and a Congressman, in light of the threat of nuclear war, in the survival of the nation, possibly the world. A therapist is involved in our psychological survival.

Our mind is so complicated, its functioning so subtle and intricate, the fantasies that influence our smallest act so many and so powerful, that a sensitive and gifted therapist with an ear finely tuned to the complexities of conflicts and the torment underlying them, is required to help us face the dangerous fantasies and strong defenses erected against acting them out.

Langs is speaking to three groups. To the public, he points out what he calls the state of "utter chaos" of psychotherapy outside of psychoanalysis. To the psychoanalysts, he is saying he believes there are a number who do not "listen" to the unconscious messages of patients in regard to the breaking of ground rules, and who sometimes make inappropriate interpretations.

To the beginning therapists who wish to become more knowledgable about psychoanalytic practice, who may have just started or completed their personal analysis, he is saying that, as part of their training, they should learn to listen to what patients are unconsciously telling therapists about their errors in regard to the breaking of ground rules and interpretations.

To the public he spells out this message: "The signs of the questionable qualities of psychotherapy are blatant yet for the most part ignored. It is an unfortunate tribute to the desperate defensive capacities of the human mind that there is so little outrage, so little concern. What is offered the patient as therapy, generally speaking, adds up to a horrifying picture. There is only the occasional cry of rebellion as a patient commits suicide or someone writes of his destructive therapeutic experience."

Patients will accept almost any therapy offered, he says, because: (1) they are desperate; (2) they prefer to work over "the therapist's madness" rather than their own; (3) they consciously deceive themselves about the quality of therapy they are receiving though unconsciously they sense its destructiveness; and (4) they do not wholeheartedly *want* to get better, they fear the pain of facing threatening feelings they have repressed and choose to stay with a therapist who does not require them to suffer this pain.

"Quick relief is what most patients come for, relief in the fastest, easiest way possible," Langs says. "And there are plenty of therapists eager and willing to oblige them, though, of course, the therapist who believes a patient can be quickly cured is acting under a delusion."

It is time for psychotherapists to be held accountable on some level for all that is done in the name of the profession, Langs asserts. There should be an end to their excuses for failure, for their rationalizing that the patient is too mentally ill to accept help. Therapists should know why *they* fail and either change technique or "get out of a profession where they are making the unhappy unhappier."

"How do you define psychotherapy?" I asked Langs.

"Psychotherapy is the treatment of an emotional disorder by psychological means," he said. "But each key word raises questions. What is 'treatment'? What is 'emotional disorder'? What are 'psychological means'?"

"First, what do you mean by treatment?"

"Treatment can involve virtually any procedure imaginable and not a few beyond common fantasy. In the name of psychotherapy a troubled person is offered sexual intercourse with the therapist or other patients in a group orgy. Or urged to express violence. Or given orders to think or act differently. Or told if he eats certain foods his mental health will improve."

"Second, what is meant by emotional disorder?"

"That's another elusive term. There exists a wide range of psychological symptoms from anxiety and panic attacks to phobias and hallucinations. There are psychosomatic syndromes such as asthma, migraine headaches and peptic ulcers, all related to emotional disturbances. Actually, emotional elements exist in all physical illnesses. The mind and body cannot be separated, much as we defensively try."

"And what are the psychological means of treatment you referred to?"

"They vary from techniques as opposite as psychoanalysis and sex therapy. The person who suffers emotionally can choose from three hundred forms of psychotherapy including creative aggression, art, group, bio, cognitive, rational-emotive, computer, crisis, holistic, logo, megativitan, music, primal, provocative, realness, rebirthing, vido, vit-Erg — just to name a few."

Langs paused, then added, "Since no specific criteria exist by which a psychotherapeutic experience can be clearly established, we might say that the present broad definition of psychotherapy as the treatment of an emotional disorder by psychological means is essentially meaningless."

Questionable forms of therapy are far more pervasive and unrecognized than in any other branch of the healing professions. "The nation has been blitzed with the psychobabble of pop psychology — everyone wants to be a counselor to a client," warned Dr. H. Keith H. Brodie in his presidential address before the psychiatrists of the nation attending the 136th annual meeting of the American Psychiatric Association in New York on May 2, 1983.

An overwhelming number of practitioners operate without basic training in the techniques of psychotherapy. Langs says, "The situation is such that virtually any person in the United States who so chooses may put out a shingle and call himself a psychotherapist. If someone is moved to consult with him, he is in practice."

A charismatic therapist can catch the public fancy and create a fad or even a school of psychotherapy that teaches "new-found" techniques. Many training programs exist with different sets of loosely defined, arbitrary standards.

Though a number of psychotherapists are charlatans, Langs believes most therapists are sincere in their desire to help. But they may be inadequately trained or ineffectively analyzed and promise help they cannot give. They have not resolved their own conflicts and show unconscious hostile or seductive behavior to patients.

The unrealistic promises of "cure" from practitioners who represent such highly different techniques as Gestalt therapy and primal scream, Langs says, "point to a situation totally out of control." That no one has taken action in behalf of patients, he attributes to what he calls "one of many conspiracies in psychotherapy, showing the willingness of patients and the public at large to submit to or accept without protest unmistakable destructive ministrations by therapists."

"Why doesn't the buyer of psychological help 'beware'?" I asked.

"Because the patient often has strong unconscious needs to find not the best but the worst therapist possible," Langs said.

"Why is that?" I was puzzled.

"So both patient and therapist can engage in collusion and a compromised treatment situation," Langs explained. "The majority of persons in psychotherapy are involved in a conspiracy with the therapist — think about that!"

"I hate to," I muttered.

"The conspiracy has as its goal the unspoken agreement that the therapist does not have to help the patient," he explained. "The 'flight into health' or temporary 'cure' of a symptom like a migraine headache or an ulcer is all the patient wants, if he is fortunate enough to get even that. The patient is all too willing to receive a bogus help that relieves his anxiety for a while. He can believe he is doing something about his life but is actually changing nothing. He will continue to suffer and end up a little more disillusioned. The pain he would have to deal with in effective therapy is terrifying. It is the last thing a patient and many a therapist wants to tackle.

"One of the great misfortunes of psychotherapy, and yet one of its great attractions, is that the client wishes as much for poor treatment as for good. Human nature, with its powerful, seemingly innate and biologically founded defensive trends, leads most in-

dividuals in the direction of least resistance. And most psychotherapists are quite human. If patients want damaged services, damaged
services they will get."

I thought of the many times on the couch I wished only for
reassurance and solace and the feeling someone cared for me, rather
than face the difficult task of exploring my deeper feelings and conflicts. As I looked back, I shed a figurative tear for the hours wasted
because I could not tackle the truths of my life. "Resistance," Freud
called it. A defensive process with the psychic quality of the rock
of Gibraltar.

In *The Psychotherapeutic Conspiracy* Langs eloquently explains why it is difficult for both patient and therapist to face head-
on the truths that underlie emotional disturbances. He says: "These
truths involve highly traumatic memories and perceptions and their
subsequent elaboration in fantasy. They involve traumas with those
whom the patient at one time or another deeply loved and who none-
theless proved to be hurtful. They entail losses that are painful to
acknowledge and the response of quiet denial. They also touch upon
inner impulses that are the source of considerable anxiety, guilt, depression, shame, and revulsion. Gaining direct access to these recol-
lection-fantasy complexes is therefore enormously disturbing.

"The inner mental basis of an emotional disturbance involves
all that is forbidden, repugnant, repulsive, primitive, and terrifying. The early nascent mental functioning of the child remains within
the adult, covered over though not entirely sealed off. On that level,
experience is fragmented, uncertain, and highly instinctualized with
both aggressive and sexual qualities. Incest is rampant, as is murder
and dismemberment. The primitive conscience operates largely by
the law of Talion: an eye for an eye, a tooth for a tooth. A murderous mutilating fantasy contains within it the threat of mutilating
punishment. A murderous mutilating unconscious perception of the
mother leads to helplessness, fear of annihilation, and fantasies of
mutilating revenge.

"In another sense, it is the helplessness, the horrible contradictions in our images of ourselves and others, the tumultuous realization that we can no longer fuse with mother and, instead, must

indeed ultimately die, which are the unconscious basis of the perceptions and conflicts that drive us crazy. Interpersonally, there are the inevitable maternal and paternal contradictions and failures. Then too there are the infuriating arrivals of siblings who will compete for affection and interfere with our own personal needs. There are also the inevitable realizations that we are by no means omnipotent, and the unavoidable disappointments and frustrations that further account for neurosis.

"To these factors, add the influence of specific conflicts, failings, disturbed self-image, and emotional problems in the parental figures, which are communicated consciously and unconsciously to the child. The perception and experience of these failings and hidden but expressed fantasies, the terror of an unconscious realization of a parent's wish to destroy his or her child, create some of the overwhelming affects that prompt the defenses we need in order to preserve our sanity and some semblance of emotional equilibrium. No one is immune. Small wonder we are all neurotic and even psychotic in some lesser or greater way. Reality and other persons will inevitably fail us, and coping efforts can never be entirely successful. The very mechanisms by which we protect ourselves — repression, denial, displacement, disguise, and other defenses — are the same means by which we become neurotic and react inappropriately to situations in our daily life.

"Conflict, defense, and compromise abound. There is the struggle between the impulse and restraint, between what we validly and painfully perceive and the need to deny, between the pressure to express our innermost fantasies and the need to cover them over, and more broadly between expression and concealment. Toward those who traumatize us, we react with mistrust and fear. While we must express our reaction to the horrors they create within ourselves, we must also insure our safety in the face of the dangers they present; we therefore seek out compromise and defense. Unconsciously, we attempt to find clever ways to react, to find revenge, to defend ourselves, while all the while maintaining innocence and affection. Intrapsychically and interpersonally neuroses arise from turmoil, chaos and pain, and out of the necessity for simultaneous expression and defense.

"Neuroses arise from the ever-present contradictions in others and in ourselves. When our defenses and other efforts at coping succeed, we get along reasonably well. When they fail, we develop symptoms that enable us to cope, though at considerable cost."

The decision to enter therapy is a momentous one. It takes courage to decide to open the self to hidden madness. We have to slowly face the childhood murderous feelings for our mother, our father and our brothers and sisters, or anyone else who made us feel rejected or temporarily abandoned. We have to confront our homosexual and incestuous and promiscuous wishes, our greed and envy and our desire to be special.

Langs uses the word "madness" for what exists in a therapist which is, in his word, "inappropriate" to treatment. He says therapists have used the word "countertransference" to intellectualize their "madness" and it is time they realize the ways in which they unconsciously displace aspects of their madness on patients "and feel challenged to change."

There are degrees of madness. The therapist who seduces a patient or is consistently sarcastic or openly hostile is at one end of Langs' scale. The therapist who is sometimes late for an appointment or asks unnecessary questions is at the other end. Though, to Langs, "madness is madness whenever it is an intervention that injures the patient."

"Why are questions harmful to the patient?" I asked, thinking of the questions of a former therapist, though never so many as those I hurled—after all, my profession was reporter, my task to ask questions. It took a long time to feel safe enough on the couch so I could talk freely, put an end to the censoring I believed necessary to be thought a little angel who never possessed an evil fantasy about anyone.

Langs answered, "If you listen to most of the questions a therapist asks, you find they have little to do with the needs of the patient. Why should a therapist ask a patient, for instance, 'Why did you do this'? as if the patient knew. The therapist should understand that the patient acts out of unconscious needs of which he is unaware. What possible reason is there for asking such questions? It derails the patient in his thoughts. It confuses him. He thinks, 'I ought to know why I did this but somehow I don't know why'. When a therapist behaves in a way to promote confusion in the patient, he unconsciously tends to drive the patient crazy. An extreme form of confusion is madness. When you can't reconcile opposing images and beliefs, you run the risk of madness."

Langs believes, "Many therapists are a long way from creating a safe therapy to protect patients from unconscious signs of the therapists' mad behavior. They give contradictory messages — the double bind of early parenting. This is what I call a 'split' in the therapist. Doing something constructive in one area, unconsciously destructive in another."

Any flaw in the relationship will create in the patient the feeling the therapist is mad and therapy is harmed, Langs says. Only if therapists protect patients against experiencing the therapists' madness are the patients able to face their own madness.

I thought of times I had left the office of a therapist muttering, "He's crazy" and in one instance, "She's crazy." Had I been right in these particular moments? I had felt injured, some sense in me protested that even granting the wildest flight of imagination what the therapist had said was not true or what the therapist had done was erratic and strange.

Langs asserted, "It's painful for a therapist to acknowledge his signs of madness. Obviously he acts unconsciously, but if he cannot face the madness, the past remains alive in both patient and therapist, haunting both."

From the moment we decide to contact a therapist, he becomes the most important figure in our lives. Because of our intense investment in the relationship, we become almost excruciatingly perceptive of every nuance in the therapist's behavior — the expression in his eyes as he greets us or bids farewell until the interminable hours end when we are once again in his office; his sighs; his restlessness in the chair; his coughs; his laughter (if any).

As Langs emphasizes again and again, when a therapist breaks a ground rule or does not provide a needed interpretation, he is experienced by the patient as fulfilling his own pathological needs and failing and traumatizing the patient in some way.

Langs claims "virtually every form of therapy in existence has practitioners who intervene by offering patients false substitutes for the truths they fail to express. These false substitutes may be fanciful dynamic and genetic formulations that have little bearing on the truth. The Gestalt therapist and Existentialist concentrate the patient in the 'here and now'. The primal scream therapist encourages the patient to express infant rage and little else. The learning therapist emphasizes 'deconditioning'."

By ignoring the conscious and unconscious communicative interaction — the means in treatment by which the truths are mobilized — the therapist never faces the underlying basis of the patient's emotional disturbance. Langs calls this "lie" therapy, using a judgmental term some critics question. Usually such a term is understood exclusively in its conscious context. Is repression the same as telling a lie? When we indulge in a lie we do so with conscious awareness. But to repress a truth and act as if it does not exist is an unconscious process. When we unconsciously displace our feelings on someone else and accuse him of a crime we wish to commit or have committed, is this the same as a conscious accusation, the critics ask?

Many patients try to convince themselves they are trying to understand the "truth" about their sickness but in reality no such effort is taking place. Langs calls this the "*I am trying (but not really) aspect of lie-barrier therapy.*"

"Lie-barrier" systems occur, he says, because while patient and therapist may have "a deep investment in the truth no matter how painful, the human mind is divided. Another investment determines our behavior and communication in more powerful fashion — investment in protective defenses, though we are not fully aware of this."

Such self-deception may provide a patient with some immediate sense of relief from symptoms, easing his physical pain, lessening aspects of guilt and self-condemnation. But the patient in "lie-barrier" therapy is never quite at peace because he substitutes a set of "fictions" for the truth about himself. The traumas of reality will require either a reinforcement of his defenses or he will suffer the reappearance of his symptoms.

A number of psychotherapists of all kinds make extensive use of clichés in the "lie-barrier" treatments they offer patients, Langs asserts. The psychoanalyst uses theoretical formulations such as penis envy, Oedipal complex and separation anxiety "in a manner totally devoid of interactional and unconscious meaning." Nonanalytic therapists fill their patients with slogans. "I'm okay, you're okay," is a prime example of "cure through cliché," Langs says.

Not only is the patient willing to accept mediocre care and engage in an unconscious conspiracy with the therapist to provide it, but the therapist, because of his personal unanalyzed pathological needs, will unconsciously use destructive feelings of hostility or seductiveness in the service of his own pathology.

"The therapist's cry for help, heard by the patient, may well allude to and convey the plight of many patients in psychotherapy today," Langs says. "Through rare direct and, more often, indirect or encoded messages, patients cry out for help when faced with a therapist who is hurtful out of his unconscious needs. The patient feels trapped in a terrifying situation from which there is no escape or relief. Remarkably few patients take flight from treatment despite a deep unconscious sense of this kind."

A female patient in her thirties remained in analysis for seven years with a prominent woman analyst in her sixties. The analyst, a widow, eventually married a younger man, telling the patient apologetically, "When you get older, you marry for companionship." The patient had often seen the younger man in the analyst's home, where one room served as an office, and had sensed the younger man was homosexual.

During the analysis, the patient started an affair with a man ten years younger than herself who, she discovered, was bisexual. When she told this to the analyst, the latter threatened to end treatment unless the patient gave up this man. Fearful the analyst would throw her out, the patient lied, said she no longer saw the younger man and never spoke of him in treatment. Desperate for help, the patient stayed seven years with this analyst, then finally left when, she later told another analyst, the strain of the song "Seven Years With the Wrong Woman" kept running through her head. The second analyst helped her understand why she had remained with the first even as she sensed the pathology in a therapist who ordered her to give up a man because he was bisexual. This patient unconsciously had copied the behavior of her analyst, just as she had, while growing up, unconsciously imitated her mother in many respects.

Virtually every form of psychotherapy reflects pathology in a number of its followers, Langs maintains, though usually not as open as the instance above. While treatment should be designed entirely for the therapeutic needs of the patient and for those satisfactions the therapist can get within the accepted confines, this is all too seldom the case, he adds.

The analyst described above broke the following ground rules: her office was in her home, where the patient saw the analyst's fiancé; the analyst made remarks about her personal life, including the death of her husband and her forthcoming marriage, as well as allusions to her fiancé's homosexuality in saying he was only a "companion"; the analyst had no right to threaten an end to the patient's treatment if she did not give up a man who was bisexual, thus encouraging the patient to lie. Both became part of a therapeutic conspiracy.

Therapists may profess one intention but unconsciously carry out another. They may believe they are healing the patient but instead attempt to heal themselves, Langs says. They offer conditions designed to create barriers to the expression of the patient's emotional disturbances and to limit the measure of meaning in the patient's words.

"While interpretations are consciously designed to explain to the patient the basis for his emotional illness, the unconscious goal of many a therapist appears to be to express a series of fictions that reveal more of the therapist's inner fantasy life and pathology than the true basis of the patient's emotional difficulty," Langs says. "Therapists claim to offer interpretations designed to help the patients understand themselves, while in actuality their interventions do not provide such insight. They intend consciously to cure through understanding, but their interventions are often expressions of unconscious wishes to be hurtful, uninsightful, or noncurative."

A number of therapists tend to have undue confidence in the validity of their interventions and seldom question themselves in the face of repudiation by the patient, Langs says: "They have a tendency to press on with their ideas and impressions, bowling over the patient, as it were, in a somewhat assaultive fashion. All too often, patients return for more."

He describes another dimension of the conspiracy as the patient's acceptance of the therapist's attitude that the patient alone is the "sick" member of the therapeutic twosome and that the therapist, by contrast, is quite healthy. In itself, the idea that the patient is ill and the therapist is healthy need not be conspiratorial. But it becomes so when the patient functions quite well and reveals a considerable capacity for sound unconscious functioning, Langs says. It is a deviation for the therapist to neglect the strengths of the patient and similarly to deny the actual reflections of sickness in his own "mistaken silences and interventions."

It was a new idea to me that patients may function unconsciously as therapists as therapists unconsciously become patients. This concept was introduced to Langs by the work of Dr. Harold Searles. Langs says, "Conspiracy may be one of victim and victimizer. It may be a means by which both patient and therapist evade painful truths, to the relief of both. The therapist functions unconsciously as the patient; the patient functions unconsciously as the therapist. While stating that he will cure the patient, the therapist unconsciously attempts to cure himself. While indicating he wishes to be cured, the patient unconsciously attempts to cure the therapist."

The patient finds immediate relief in sensing that the treatment focuses unconsciously on the illness of the therapist, Langs explains. By not having to face his sickness (like not having to face surgery), the patient feels temporarily comforted. In the case cited above, the female patient was carrying out the analyst's unconscious wishes through the patient's involvement with a bisexual, giving approval of the analyst's involvement with a homosexual. Consciously, however, the analyst could not tolerate this act in a patient and threatened to end treatment.

Langs points out that such a therapist, one afforded "the honored position of the healer," engages in a sanctioned technique through which important aspects of his own pathology are expressed. While consciously dedicated to the cure of the patient, such a therapist becomes unconsciously involved in the cure of his own emotional ills, and imposes thoughts, feelings and fantasies on the treatment.

"Such a therapist believes he is interpreting the meaning of the patient's material and identifying the patient's unconscious messages but instead uses his own fabrications and fictional systems to cover over and avoid the underlying truths in the patient's communications," Langs says. "This is madness."

Langs maintains that patients often consciously feel somewhat cured in therapy if they believe they are no madder than the therapist. Unconscious perceptions of the conflicts and unconscious wishes of the therapist convey a sense to the patient that his sickness is not uniquely "bad" and "unpardonable," making him feel different from everyone else, if the therapist suffers in kind. "The therapist becomes less of a threat," Langs explains. "How comforting indeed, even if it occurs unconsciously, for the patient to realize his therapist is, in significant ways, no better off than he is. It takes the sting out of being emotionally ill. The therapist is no longer a god but a human being. This may prove temporarily beneficial to the patient, though it is no cure."

Another temporary curative factor, comforting because it relates to the familial and familiar, lies in the patient's finding out that the pathology of the therapist is similar to the pathology of the patient's mother or father. Langs says, "Because of this, the sick therapist becomes a basis for forgiving or coming to some kind of terms with the emotionally sick parent. The patient's relationship with his parents may become less hostile."

One woman stayed with what she sensed a very disturbed, attacking therapist who was much like her father. "In learning how to handle a verbally assaultive person (therapist and father), she coped better with reality, was actually able to become more creative," Langs says. "Another reason for conspiracies is that some respond to trauma and adversity with adaptive and innovative reactions, though this too is no cure."

In the psychotherapeutic conspiracy, the therapist takes his own statements to the patient at face value. The therapist believes that what he means to say has been communicated consciously and "there is a strong denial of his unconscious messages to the patient and the patient's hidden messages to him," Langs points out.

He calls the therapist "the main perpetrator of harm and distortion within the conspiracy," with the patient as "the willing victim." The conspiracy is largely outside the awareness of both participants. At the heart of the conspiracy lies "a deep and abiding dread of the

underlying truths of the patient's neurosis and of the emotional illness of the therapist as well. The realizations involved seem so terrifying that relief through virtually any other means than the truth
is preferred by patient and therapist alike. Collusion and conspiracy
are therefore inevitable."

Even though taking part in this collusion, the patient unconsciously "knows the terrible truths of the underlying conspiracy,"
Langs asserts. "It is one of the remarkable capabilities of the human
mind to divide its knowledge, understanding, and perceptions into
those that are conscious and those that are unconscious. This split
is often merciful and spares much pain. At other times, it places us
in highly self-destructive situations we accept on the surface, though
we sense their detrimental qualities unconsciously. Ironically, the
very mental mechanisms that protect us from being overwhelmed
emotionally and enable us to cope are the same ones that divide the
self and create mental illness."

Psychoanalysis began with a psychotherapeutic conspiracy,
according to Langs. Freud was not the therapist but Dr. Josef Breuer,
a physician and internist. Breuer told Freud of his success in clearing
up the hysterical symptoms of a young woman he hypnotized (later
revealed by Dr. Ernest Jones in the biography of Freud as Bertha
Pappenheim). Breuer, reporting on her case for the book he wrote
jointly with Freud, *Studies on Hysteria*, published in 1895, called his
patient Anna O. to protect her identity.

As the family physician, Breuer was called to the home of the
Pappenheim family in December 1880, when Freud was still a medical
student, to treat their twenty-one-year-old daughter. After nursing
her dying father for four months, she had fallen into a psychotic
state in which she suffered hallucinations, muteness, language disorders, altered states of consciousness she called "clouds," suicidal
wishes and paralysis of her limbs. She could hardly see, coughed
incessantly and refused food.

At that time there was little in the way of therapy for emotional
problems other than hypnotism, rest, electroshock, massage, seda-
tives and morphine. There was no understanding of the psychological cause of emotional illness.

When Breuer first saw Anna O., she was confined to bed in

a room next to the one in which her wealthy father lay dying from a lung abscess. At the time Breuer was thirty-nine. By his own description, he found his sick patient a highly sympathetic, intellectually stimulating (as she recovered), attractive young woman. He persuaded her to eat, fed her, hypnotized her and listened to her outpourings of fairy tales and highly imaginative stories in which she spoke of a young girl anxiously sitting by a sickbed.

Breuer discovered she felt greatly relieved as she talked. He visited her every day, sometimes twice a day, and slowly became aware that a series of traumatic experiences were connected to each of her physical symptoms. He encouraged her to recall in detail the specific occasion on which she first experienced a symptom, and when she came out of the hypnotic trance, the symptom had disappeared. She called this "the talking cure," described it as "chimney sweeping."

For instance, during the summer of 1881, in spite of great thirst, she had been unable to drink liquids. One day, under hypnosis, she spoke of a new English companion she disliked. With a strong feeling of disgust, she described going into the woman's room and observing a little dog drinking out of a glass. She had said nothing, holding back her disgust and rage. But when she released her angry feelings under hypnosis, she was able to drink water.

Her nervous cough disappeared after she recalled standing by the side of her father's bed one summer night, listening to an orchestra in the house next door, as couples danced at a party to which she had been invited. She told Breuer she had started to cough as she stood at the window, wishing she were at the party, resenting having to perform nursing duties for her father.

"Guided by the perceptiveness of his patient, and brilliantly perceptive in his own right, Josef Breuer was the first physician to listen to the thoughts of a very emotionally ill person and find they contained hidden meanings," Langs points out. "He was the first physician to attempt to trace these meanings to the patient's recent life, though not to her childhood. The discovery of hidden meanings beneath hysterical paralysis, coughs and other symptoms was a monumental breakthrough. The development of a cure by having the patient describe and vent, or 'abreact' feelings connected with experiences and their implications was even more staggering. In a stroke, the hidden or unconscious basis of emotional illness and its roots in earlier traumas were discovered — momentous findings indeed."

Breuer, who completed the treatment of Anna O. in June of 1882, when all her physical symptoms had disappeared, said nothing of this experience to anyone until he confided it to Freud in November of that year. Freud later guessed Breuer had terminated the treatment abruptly when one day he found Anna O. in a confused state, writhing with abdominal cramps — in the throes of a phantom pregnancy in which she imagined the baby's father was Breuer. Just prior to this, he told her he would have to end treatment. It was later reported that his wife was jealous of the time and attention he had given the younger woman and his incessant talk of her at home.

Based on what is known, Langs says, Breuer and Anna O. "opened the door to a variety of psychotherapeutic methods on the basis of an intriguing combination of healthy and unhealthy motives and efforts. There appear several collusive aspects to this remarkable discovery of the 'talking cure'. There are suggestions that both Anna O. and Breuer had a special interest and involvement in the relationship they had developed."

The first collusion was to engage in therapy as a cover for, and secret expression of, a mutual attraction. Though Breuer was almost forty, double the age of Anna O., and had five children, he evidently found Anna O. very attractive, as his wife's jealousy attested. Anna O.'s phantom pregnancy was not all in her mind; she no doubt sensed his attraction to her. Another conspiracy, one of silence, was designed to leave out the personal interaction between patient and therapist. Breuer reported in his description of the case that she never mentioned sex and seemed completely asexual, as he denied any sexual factor in her illness. This silence was maintained almost to the end when she broke it by the phantom pregnancy, as though saying to him there was indeed a sexual aspect, even though unconscious, to the treatment.

Many forms of present-day psychotherapy also conspire to ignore the relationship between patient and therapist, pretend nothing is happening between them, Langs asserts. "While the degree of denial is massive, its use is extremely common," he says. "Breuer's collusion with Anna O., the first psychotherapy patient, has provided a heritage carried forward to this day."

Collusion and denial are vital for patients and therapists who cannot tolerate the open expression — or derivative communication — of sexual and aggressive fantasies and perceptions, Langs says, especially as they apply to the other member of the therapeutic twosome: "To this day, countless therapists dread the contents of the unconscious part of the mind. They fear the highly sensitive perceptions patients unconsciously have of them and the ways in which their own innermost secrets are revealed in how they work with patients. They fear the primitive qualities of the patient's inner mental life and imagination. They create misalliances with their patients that are designed to exclude all such realizations in their communications."

Breuer, knowing or sensing the truth, that he was deeply involved emotionally with his patient and in a subtle sense had seduced her, found what he had done intolerable and fled. Freud, with his patients, somehow aware of his seductiveness and its influence in therapy, remained. Langs asks, "How was Freud able to do so?" And answers: "Freud seems to have built up, perhaps through early efforts at self-analysis or through his own natural and evolved propensities, a capacity to tolerate from his patients relatively open expressions of sexuality. It may well be that in reality he experienced little conscious attraction to the women with whom he worked. There is evidence Freud was attracted to hysterical women. There are also signs he tended to deny this attraction with defenses that did not always hold. Freud's great sense of distance from his women patients seems to have served him well in his initial efforts to probe more deeply into their inner mental worlds."

Langs adds: "Freud was not devoid of sexual feelings and fantasies, he simply managed better to defend himself against their expression. It seems likely that Freud did not have Breuer's problems in dealing with conscious erotic feelings and reactions. As Freud said to Martha, when she expressed concern that, like Breuer, he might become emotionally involved with a woman patient, 'For that, one has to be a Breuer.' To be a Freud, erotic fantasies and feelings about patients were subjected to rigid or effective defenses and remained mostly outside of consciousness."

It is in the nature of the human mind to have fantasies that are sexual and the difference between a Breuer and a Freud is one of "manifest expression," Langs notes, where "the difference between health and pathology is one of control, management, understanding and the use of healthy defenses so that the underlying fantasies do not interfere with functioning or daily life."

Given the intimacy of the therapeutic relationship, sexual and aggressive stirrings are "absolutely inevitable," Langs says. A therapist has no choice but to be aware of them or deny them. Some therapists interpret a patient's sexual feelings in terms of the transference alone, others try to understand their own part in the interaction by listening to the patient's free associations that show the therapist as seductive or hostile.

The manner in which a therapist consciously deals with his own erotic and hostile feelings and fantasies aroused by a patient "is a major determinant of the therapeutic measures used both in the field at large and in regard to the personal choice of each individual therapist," Langs says. "It is also a key factor in the nature of the psycho-therapeutic conspiracy that a therapist offers a patient. The use of transference — blaming everything on the patient — serves as a protective barrier between the therapist's conscious awareness and his inner stirrings. The use of transference supports a therapist's defensiveness without his truly understanding the patient."

Because of the enormity of the threats involved in knowing the truth about the self, it may well be that there never would have been a psychoanalytic movement were it not for the defensive use of the concept of transference, Langs says, whereby the therapist can deny he is to blame for errors in technique. There is every indication, Langs maintains, that the underlying truths of a patient's emotional disturbance, as constituted by both threatening fantasies and threatening perceptions of the therapist, "are more disturbing than most minds can bear. Patients can experience these truths only if they are relatively disguised. Therapists have required some way of muting these truths lest they too go mad."

That collusion and conspiracy are rampant within the field of psychotherapy "is a staggering and disturbing realization in the face of the knowledge that true growth and development, personal and professional, can take place only within a treatment that embodies painful honesty on the part of both patient and therapist," Langs says.

He adds, "Since psychoanalysis strives to arrive at both conscious and unconscious truths and attempts to take into account both surface and deeper phenomena, it alone appears the discipline from which the truth will emerge."

8
THE CLASSICAL
ROOTS

To understand Langs is also to know the bedrock of classical theory about technique, on which his work rests — the concepts of transference and countertransference. To a patient they mean nothing, for they are the psychological tools of the therapist. But if they are not kept sharp, as Langs warns, the patient will not be able to face his inner life.

Langs has edited *Classics in Psychoanalytic Technique,* which comprises forty-three historic articles about transference and countertransference, with introductions by Langs describing the article's significance in the development of psychoanalytic technique. He has also abstracted more than five hundred articles from psychoanalytic literature that appear in two large volumes, *The Therapeutic Interaction.*

Langs accepts Freud's theory of transference, though the communicative approach has shown, he says, that Freud used transference as a way of defending against "non-transference" — unconscious and conscious feelings aroused by the patient. But by discovering the very presence of powerful unconscious forces within the therapeutic relationship, Freud started the investigation of what Langs calls the "spiralling communicative interaction" between patient and therapist.

As early as 1895, Freud indicates his awareness of transference and how the manner of the analyst may affect transference in a negative way. This observation appears in *Studies on Hysteria,* where Freud points out that the analyst makes the patient a collaborator and the treatment may fail if the patient's relationship to the physician is disturbed. Freud calls transference "the greatest obstacle" to psychoanalysis when the relationship is disturbed but the "powerful ally" if "its presence can be detected each time and explained to the patient." He also says that, at times, a physician's "friendliness" is needed as a substitute for love. Langs points out that Freud was known for his friendliness to most patients though, with some, he could not conceal his dislike.

Freud describes three main instances in which the analyst may have difficulty with a patient. First, there may be a personal estrangement based on the patient's feeling he is neglected, unappreciated or insulted, or has heard unfavorable comments about the physician. Second, there may be a dread within the patient of becoming too accustomed to the physician personally and of losing her (most of his patients at this time were women) independence, or possibly becoming sexually dependent (in a sublimated way) on him. Freud calls this the result of the special solicitude inherent in the treatment and notes it creates a new motive for resistance within the patient and is shown during every effort at therapy.

In the third instance, Freud mentions transference. It occurs when the patient becomes "frightened at finding that she is transferring onto the figure of the physician the distressing ideas which arise from the content of the analysis." He adds that transference takes place through a *"false connection,"* which he calls a *"més-alliance"* (Langs speaks of it as "misalliance").

Ten years later, in 1905, publishing his famous Dora case, "Fragment of an Analysis of a Case of Hysteria," Freud reports aspects of the treatment of an eighteen-year old girl. His main interest in the case was to validate his technique in interpreting a dream. In a later edition he admits in a postscript to the case that he had neglected analyzing Dora's current conflicts, especially her relationship to him. He describes their rather rocky relationship as a major factor in her decision to end the analysis after eleven weeks.

In this article he defines transference as "new additions or facsimiles of the impulses and phantasies which are aroused and made conscious during the progress of the analysis." These additions have a "peculiarity," he says, in that "they replace some earlier person by the person of the physician. To put it another way: whole series of psychological experiences are revived, not as belonging to the past, but as applying to the person of the physician at the present moment."

Psychoanalytic treatment does not "create" transference but merely brings it to light, along with other hidden psychic factors, Freud says. All the patient's feelings, including the hostile ones, are aroused, then used for the purpose of analysis by being made conscious, so that transference is constantly being created and destroyed.

Five years later, in 1910, Freud introduced the term "countertransference" in his article, "The Future Prospects of Psycho-analytic Therapy." He says: "We have become aware of the 'counter-transference' which arises in him [the physician] as a result of his patient's influence on his unconscious feelings." Stressing the need to overcome this countertransference, Freud says no analyst can go further in his work than his own complexes and resistances permit. He advocates self-analysis to overcome the resistances.

In 1912, in "Recommendations to Physicians Practising Psychoanalysis," Freud suggests technical rules for psychoanalysis based on his clinical experience. It is here he says the analyst should model himself after the surgeon, who puts aside all feelings, including human sympathy, and concentrates on performing his operation as skillfully as possible.

In an eloquent passage, Heinrich Racker, a psychoanalyst from South America, in his book *Transference and Countertransference* published in 1968, discusses Freud's advice that the analyst should be a "mirror." Racker says he believes Freud gave this advice because of the habit, prevalent among some analysts of that early period, of relating facts of their lives to patients. Racker says, "Freud was telling all analysts to speak to the patient only of himself."

Racker writes: "'Be a mirror' . . . did not mean 'stop being of flesh and blood and transform yourself into glass covered with silver nitrate.' The positive intention of not showing more than the indispensable of one's own person does not have to be carried as far as to deny (or even inhibit), in front of the patient, the analyst's interest and affection towards him. For only Eros can originate Eros. And this is what matters in the last instance, when thinking of the aim of analysis which is the new putting into action of the rejected libido, as well as when considering the decisive role played by the positive transference, or considering working through the 'depressive position' which can only be attained by means of an increase of Eros."

Just as the positive transference is of fundamental importance for analytic work, Racker asserts, so is the positive countertransference and "its full unfolding through the hard work the analyst must do to understand and interpret. Only in this way, in the analytic situation, can really favorable *climate* be created for the work to be done. The analyst's relation to his patient *is* a libidinal one, and is a constant emotional experience; the analyst's desires, frustrations, and anxieties are real, however slight; and the countertransference in part constantly oscillates with the oscillations of the transference, and the therapeutic outcome depends to a large extent on the analyst's capacity to maintain his positive countertransference over and above his 'countertransference neurosis'; or else, to free it again and again from any harm it may have suffered, just like the Phoenix, which always rises again from its own ashes."

Racker points out that the analyst's "different internal attitudes" towards the patient's material determine different techniques. "At bottom this also involves the analyst's different attitudes towards himself," Racker explains. "Unconscious anxieties in face of certain aspects of one's own unconscious give rise to anxieties in face of the patient's unconscious, and lead to diverse defensive measures which interfere with one's work; for instance, creating excessive distance, rigidity, coldness, difficulty in giving free course to associations and feelings within one's self, and inhibited behavior towards the patient. In this case, as well as in the opposite one, in which the analyst is 'flooded' by his unconscious, the transference and countertransference neurosis may become dominant in the analytic situation; the positive transference and countertransference (which in better circumstances gain strength from the real analytic situation) recede, and this in a degree greater than what is convenient for therapy, since any analytic work, any communication, and any understanding — i.e., any union — spring from these positive feelings."

Racker then encourages the analyst to examine the free associations, fantasies and feelings that arise in response to the patient's material, for only then "can the analyst, for instance, reproduce the concrete fantasies which the patient feels at bottom (but which are repressed and blocked)."

What Racker calls the "analytic transformation process" depends, he sums up, to a large extent, "on the quantity and quality of Eros the analyst is able to put into action for his patient. It is a specific form of Eros, it is the Eros called understanding, and it is, too, a specific form of understanding. It is, above all, the understanding of what is rejected, of what is feared and hated in the human being, and this thanks to a greater fighting strength, a greater *aggression*, against everything which conceals the truth, against illusion and denial—in other words, against man's fear and hate towards himself, and their pathological consequences."

Racker concludes: "The patient can only be expected to accept the re-experiencing of childhood if the analyst is prepared to accept fully his new paternity, to admit fully affection for his new children, and to struggle for a new and better childhood, calling upon all the available mental forces. His task consists ideally in a constant and lively interest and continuous empathy with the patient's psychological happenings, in a metapsychological analysis of every mental expression and movement, his principal attention and energy being directed towards understanding the transference (towards the always present 'new childhood') and overcoming its pathological aspects by means of adequate interpretations."

Freud also said in his 1912 paper on recommendations to physicians practicing psychoanalysis that they should not take notes because it created detrimental selections, though he accepts the occasional writing down of dates and dreams. The analyst should make use of everything the patient tells him for the purposes of interpretation without invoking any censorship. He "must turn his own unconscious like a receptive organ toward the transmitting unconscious of the patient" and may not tolerate resistances within himself that hold back from his consciousness what has been perceived by his unconscious. Unresolved repressions will create blind spots in his analytic perception, Freud warns. The analyst should continue the analytic examination of his own personality through a self-analysis so he does not give way to the temptation of projecting on the patient peculiarities of his own personality, thereby creating an erroneous theory. (Langs could say this no more strongly.)

Freud suggests here that the analyst not discuss details of his personal life, for this creates an insatiable wish in the patient to reverse the situation into the analysis of the doctor. Self-revelations also make the resolution of the transference more difficult, he adds.

Freud also advises the analyst to curb his wish to engage in educative activities with the patient. He cautions against setting tasks for the patient, such as asking the patient to collect memories or concentrate on a specific problem. Analytic writings, he says, should not be recommended to patients, the focus should be on learning through personal experience.

A year later, in 1913, in "On Beginning the Treatment (Further Recommendations on the Technique of Psycho-analysis)," Freud delineates further ground rules. He describes his use of provisional and trial periods of treatment for reasons of diagnosis. He suggests the analyst not become involved in lengthy preliminary discussions before treatment starts, noting the patient meets the doctor with a transference attitude already established, one that must be slowly uncovered. He warns two special difficulties arise when friendship exists between two patients of a given analyst. He also cautions analysts that patients expect of analysis gratification of the most boundless demands.

On matters relating to time, he advocates a definite hour that is the responsibility of the patient. He suggests that absences and illnesses are often based on resistances, which have to be analyzed. He advocates six sessions a week to keep pace with the patient's real life. Analysis is a long-term undertaking and of this the patient has to be informed. The patient is permitted to end whenever he chooses, though Freud indicates this is not as great a problem as inducing the patient to give up analysis.

He notes that the analyst's fee has both realistic and neurotic meanings, the latter related to power and sexuality. He suggests payments be made monthly and the patient not be permitted to owe large sums. He advises against free treatment because of the sacrifice it means to the analyst and the marked increased in neurotic resistances that occur in the patient. The latter feels over-grateful which hides hostile feelings.

Any indication on the part of the patient that he cannot think of anything to say is to be treated as a resistance and analyzed. Silences, as well as everything connected to the analytic situation, represent transference. As to the timing of interventions, they should wait until an effective transference is established and there is rapport between analyst and patient.

Freud deals fully with the erotic feelings of a patient for the analyst and the danger it will inflict on the patient if the analyst becomes sexually involved, in his 1915 paper, "Observations on Transference-Love (Further Recommendations on the Technique of Psycho-analysis)." The most serious difficulties in undertaking psychoanalysis lie in the management of the transference, he warns, and cites the woman who falls in love with her analyst. Freud rejects the idea of any response by the analyst through an illicit love relationship, marriage or the termination of the analysis. The situation is best viewed, he advises, as a warning in regard to the analyst's countertransference. The analyst has to recognize that "the patient's falling in love is induced by the analytic situation and is not to be attributed to the charms of his own person." Langs has noted that Freud showed unconscious wisdom in realizing something in the analysis was stimulating transference but then showed a defensiveness in saying that the "situation" was to blame, not the analyst.

Freud suggests that the analyst's response, when a patient declares her love for him, be based on sound analytic technique, involving neither rejection nor acceptance, since the patient will take revenge for either. The analyst must maintain his neutrality and keep his countertransference in check. He must deny the patient all erotic satisfaction. The rule of abstinence must hold, it is a fundamental principle of psychoanalysis that "the patient's need and longing should be allowed to persist in her, in order that they may serve as forces impelling her to do work and to make changes, and that we must beware of appeasing these forces by means of surrogates." Compliance ensures the domination of the analyst by the patient. As Freud says, "The patient would achieve *her* aim, but he would never achieve *his*." All possibility of correcting the pathological reactions of the patient's erotic life would disappear.

"The more plainly the analyst lets it be seen that he is proof against every temptation, the more readily will he be able to extract from the situation its analytic content," Freud stated. This enables the patient to feel safe enough to allow fantasies and dangerous feelings to unfold. Any gratification of the patient's erotic feelings by the analyst, he said, will preclude the eventual resolution of the patient's infantile fixations and the chance for mature love after treatment. However highly the analyst may prize the love, he must prize more highly the opportunity to help the patient over a decisive stage in life.

Freud also deals in this paper with the "quick cure" therapies by saying that "to believe that the psychoneuroses are to be conquered by operating with harmless little remedies is grossly to underestimate those disorders both as to their origin and their practical importance." The analytic resolution cannot come "without a strictly regular, undiluted psychoanalysis which is not afraid to handle the most dangerous mental impulses and to obtain mastery over them for the benefit of the patient."

In a chapter of his book, *Introductory Lectures on Psycho-Analysis,* published in 1917,Freud describes the development and nature of what he named the "transference neurosis." He notes that after a while the whole of the patient's illness is centered on a new, artificial neurosis, concentrated on his relation to the analyst. This is a "transference neurosis" that has taken the place of the earlier illness. As a result, the patient's symptoms abandon their original meaning and take on a new sense in relation to the transference. It is the mastery of this new artificial neurosis that coincides with getting rid of the illness. A person who becomes normal in relation to the analyst will remain so in his own life after the analysis ends.

Recalling my own analysis, I thought how the transference neurosis mastery occurs in slow stages, no magic in analysis, just the tortoise-paced painful look at the self as reflected in the relationship with the analyst.

Freud again warned the analyst against in any way gratifying the patient erotically in "Lines of Advances in Psycho-Analytic Therapy" in 1919. This was written after suggestions by his colleague Dr. Sandor Ferenczi that analysts show occasional friendship and affection for the patient by hugging, embracing or kissing. Freud also warned against alloying "the pure gold of analysis freely with the copper of direct suggestion," alluding to analysts who gave advice.

It was Freud's genius to know something was going on interactionally in the treatment that was vital to outcome, Langs says. Freud understood unconscious communication. He also recognized the critical importance of the patient-analyst relationship both in analytic work and the outcome of the analysis. Freud stressed the importance of interpretation of the ground rules, of the role of introjects, of the existence of a therapeutic alliance, and of a special way of listening to the patient. Freud's basic ground rules included listening attitudes, on which Langs has elaborated.

Five years before Freud died, an important contribution to the understanding of transference came from one of his analysands, James Strachey. It was the only paper Strachey ever wrote. The brother of Lytton Strachey, looking for his own niche in life, James went to Freud for a two-year analysis, as did his wife Alix. Strachey was later accepted as a member of the British Psychoanalytic Society.

To Strachey, Langs says, he owes a clear sense of the role of interaction, of unconscious communication and of interpretation based on adaptive context. These concepts are contained in Strachey's article, "The Nature of the Therapeutic Action of Psychoanalysis," published in 1934 in the *International Journal of Psycho-Analysis.*

In discussing transference, which Freud described as the battlefield on which all the mutually struggling forces in the patient met, Strachey states that, in addition to displacements from the past onto the analyst, projection onto him of the patient's current inner mental world played an important role. Also, introjection (taking in psychologically the ideas, attitudes and unconscious wishes of the analyst) had to be accorded more importance in the analytic experience.

He coined the term "mutative interpretation" to describe an intervention in which some aspect of the transference is interpreted in terms of a current emotional investment (a wish from the id — erotic or hostile) by the patient in the analyst. Strachey thus laid the basis for the understanding of how intellectual insight based on interpretations, due to the power of transference, could combine with the interactional experience to bring about inner change. This is the model for Langs' adaptive context. Strachey referred to the emotional investment as an active wish in the patient. Langs believes this wish is stimulated by the analyst creating in the patient an unconscious perception of the analyst, followed by the wish.

Strachey also spoke of what he called "the neurotic vicious circle" which analysis attempts to halt so the patient does not endlessly repeat the traumatic past. This is achieved in analysis by helping the patient become less frightened of his severe conscience and the dangerous figures of childhood, as he loses hostility towards the latter. Strachey explained: "The object [the parent] which he [the patient] then introjected [taken in psychologically] would in turn be less savage in its pressure upon the id-impulses, which would be able to lose something of their primitive ferocity. In short a *benign* circle would be set up instead of the vicious one, and ultimately the patient's libidinal development would proceed to the genital level, when, as in the case of a normal adult, his superego will be comparatively mild and his ego will have a relatively undistorted contact with reality."

An article by Melanie Klein in 1952, "The Origins of Transference," appearing in the *International Journal of Psycho-Analysis*, deserves a special place in the history of the concept of transference, Langs believes. It focuses on transference as a form of object relationship that has preoedipal as well as oedipal roots, a relationship expressed in both erotic and hostile fantasies. Langs calls her article "a wellspring for both classical Freudian and Kleinian psychoanalysts in their attempts at further clarification of the concept of transference and countertransference."

The main idea he received from Klein, Langs says, is the importance of the therapeutic interaction in relation to what she described as transference — *every* communication from the patient. He translated this into the concept that every communication from the patient has to do with therapeutic interaction, whether transference or not. That is, every communication from the patient alludes on some level both to the patient and the past and to some aspect of his relationship with the analyst.

Klein believes transference originates in the same processes which in the earliest stages of life determine the relationship between mother and baby. Thus, the patient returns again and again in analysis to the fluctuations between important persons, love and hatred, external and internal, which dominate early infancy. She emphasizes the role of aggression and the tendency of the patient to split off the aggression in order to preserve the idealization of the analyst (as he once did his mother) within the transference.

Thus Klein offers a concept of transference rooted in the earliest stages of development, in the deepest layers of the unconscious part of the mind. She suggests the analyst search for unconscious elements of the transference in all of the patient's communications, including references to everyday life and outside relationships. She also suggests study of the ways in which a patient turns away from the analyst, much as the patient did from the mother of infancy, splitting the relationship to the analyst into "good" and "bad."

Klein does not neglect later relationships but emphasizes that exploration of a full transference will include distortions from every stage of development. She describes this as a slow and painstaking process in which links to the past are made again and again. The result diminishes anxiety and guilt and synthesizes love and hate, modifying the splitting and repressive processes so the ego can gain strength as cleavage between the idealized and persecutory objects of childhood diminishes.

Winnicott wrote of interaction and of the positive functions of the ground rules, making it clear he thought the analyst contributed something other than interpretations. Freud and the American analysts emphasized interpretation rather than the relationship between analyst and patient, whereas the British, first Strachey, then Klein, then Winnicott, focused on the concept that the relationship was the important thing and, if handled properly, could be curative. Langs believes that interpretations can be used effectively by the patient if the relationship is sound, and that the relationship can be used by the patient only if the therapist is interpreting effectively.

For the patient experiences the positive "taking-in" psychologically of the therapist only when the therapist is interpreting or managing the ground rules constructively — when the frame is not contradicting an interpretation. For instance, when a therapist interprets the concept of becoming aware of but not acting out aggression, if the therapist shows signs of anger in his voice or manner, the patient will not be able to face and control his aggression.

In Winnicott's article, "The Theory of the Parent-Infant Relationship," published in 1960 in the *International Journal of Psycho-Analysis*, he traces the development of the mother-infant relationship through the child's psychic journey from absolute dependence through relative dependence to independence. In exploring the development of the child's inherited potentials and the importance of the maternal care that either facilitated or disturbed development, Winnicott described such care as including the mother's "holding" phase — the period when the mother and infant are practically alone together — and the later stage when the father is added.

Winnicott indicates that "holding" provides the special form of loving in which the ego is formed. It denotes not only the physical holding of the infant but also the total environmental atmosphere prior to the infant's concept of "living with." Winnicott calls "holding" a "spatial" relationship to which "time" is gradually added. It includes the management of developmental processes in living and takes place in a complex psychological field within which the awareness and empathy of the mother are crucial. The infant's anxiety at this stage is experienced as annihilation if his mother neglects or abuses him. Winnicott indicates important parallels between the "holding" type of maternal care and the functioning of the analyst, especially in the treatment of borderline and psychotic patients.

Prior to Langs, José Bleger was the only analyst to write in depth on the functions of ground rules. He borrowed from Winnicott's work, extending it to an analysis of the functions of the ground rules, which was then further developed by Langs. In Bleger's article of 1967, "Psycho-analysis of the Psychoanalytic Frame," appearing in the *International Journal of Psycho-Analysis*, Bleger defined the "setting" of the analysis as all the details of its management by the analyst. He applied the term "psycho-analytic situation" to "the totality of phenomena included in the therapeutic relationship between the analyst and the patient."

The "situation" included process and nonprocess. The latter

was the "frame," formed of "constants" within whose bounds the process of analysis takes place. The process itself can be examined only when the "constants" are retained. They include space (atmosphere), time factors and parts of technique (fees, interruptions). The frame provides a protection to the patient. It forms part of the steady relationship with objects and institutions out of which the ego is built. It has a strong basis in the bodily ego and in the early symbiosis between mother and child, Bleger believed.

He asserted that if this steady frame varies, the contents of the analysis will vary radically. The frame contains the symbiotic elements of the patient-analyst relationship acting as a support and mainstay; it intrudes only when it changes or breaks.

Analyst and patient bring to analysis different anticipations regarding the frame, Bleger said. The patient attempts at times to have the analyst modify the frame and repeat the neurotic interactions of childhood. If the analyst respects the frame, this repetition does not occur and the secure frame brings to life what Bleger calls the patient's "ghost world or 'psychotic core'." Only the maintenance of the frame will lead the analyst to the psychotic part of the patient's personality, a sector apart from the ego, that shapes the neurotic transference. Bleger describes two frames: one is suggested and adhered to by the analyst and consciously accepted by the patient, the other is the "ghost world" which the patient projects, part of the repetition compulsion.

Langs says the work of Dr. Merton M. Gill and Dr. Harold Searles comes closest to the concepts he has originated. Searles stresses the unconscious perceptions of the patient in the interaction of therapy and Gill emphasizes the "here and now" as stimulus for the patient's free associations, similar to Langs' adaptive context. Gill traces what patients speak of to transference whereas Langs makes a distinction between the patient's perceptions and his distortions, between transference and nontransference elements.

Gill, a psychiatrist and psychoanalyst on the staff of the Abraham Lincoln School of Medicine of the Chicago Medical Center, wrote on "The Analysis of the Transference," published by the *Journal of the American Psychoanalytic Association* in 1979. He stressed analytic interaction and said the analyst's attitudes and interventions were the stimuli for the patient's transference reactions and played a critical role within the analytic situation.

One reason for the failure of therapists to deal adequately with transference is that "it involves both analyst and patient in the most affect-laden and potentially disturbing interactions," he stated. "Both participants in the analytic situation are motivated to avoid these interactions. Flight away from the transference and to the past can be a relief to both patient and analyst."

All transference has a connection with something in the analytic situation, Gill says. There are important resistances on the part of both patient and analyst to the awareness of these connections. On the patient's part, this occurs because of the difficulty in becoming aware of erotic and hostile impulses toward the very person to whom they must be disclosed as part of cure. On the analyst's part, "because the patient is likely to attribute the very attitudes to him which are most likely to cause him discomfort . . . the attitudes the patient ascribes to the analyst are often attitudes the patient feels the analyst will not like and be uncomfortable about having ascribed to him."

Gill warns, "It is for this reason that the analyst must be especially alert to the attitudes the patient believes he has, not only to the attitudes the patient does have toward him. If the analyst is able to see himself as a participant in an interaction . . . he will become much more attuned to this important area of transference, which might otherwise escape him."

Shifting from the patient's relationship to the analyst to the analyst's relationship to the patient, this concept's heritage begins with Freud when he coined the word "countertransference" in 1910. One of the first to explore the meanings of countertransference was Paula Heimann, a British psychoanalyst. Prior to her work, countertransference was seen as pathological, as "bad," something the therapist had to get rid of. But she claimed the analyst's subjective feelings, even when pathological and distorted, were a reaction to the patient's material and could be used to understand the patient.

She introduced her ideas in a paper, "On Countertransference," presented in 1949 at the 16th International Psycho-Analytical

Congress in Zurich. She said that countertransference had not been sufficiently stressed, "that the analytic situation was a *relationship* between two persons." She noted as a danger to the relationship the analyst imputing to the patient feelings and thoughts that belonged to the analyst.

She stated: "What distinguishes this relationship from others is not the presence of feelings in one partner, the patient, and their absence in the other, the analyst, but above all, the degree of the feelings experienced and the use made of them, these factors being interdependent. . . . If an analyst tries to work without consulting his feelings, his interpretations are poor."

Declaring that the basic assumption of psychoanalysis is that the analyst's unconscious mind understands the unconscious mind of the patient, she said, "This rapport on the deep level comes to the surface in the form of feelings which the analyst notices in his 'counter-transference' . . . the most dynamic way in which his patient's voice reaches him."

Heimann suggested that if the analyst, in his personal analysis, worked through infantile conflicts and anxieties, "he will not impute to his patient what belongs to himself. He will have achieved a dependable equilibrium which enables him to carry the roles of the patient's id, ego, superego and external objects which the patient allots to him or — in other words — projects on him, when he dramatizes his conflicts in the analytic relationship."

Langs credits Heimann as the source of the concept of unconscious communication between patient and analyst and the concept of unconscious understanding, as well as the first understanding that there could be constructive use of the analyst's feelings toward the patient.

Two years later, in 1951, Dr. Margaret Little wrote "Counter-Transference and the Patient's Response to It," published in the *International Journal of Psycho-Analysis*. Langs describes her article as "filled with insights into the analytic interaction, many of them largely unappreciated even to this day."

She pointed out that at times patients made unconscious interpretations to analysts about their errors. Langs says he owes to her the recognition that analysts sometimes became patients, that patients tried to help analysts, a forerunner of Searles' concept that patients do not merely free associate but are capable of functioning in a variety of ways in the analytic situation.

Little maintained that the process of psychoanalysis had been held up for more than ten years through the analysts' fear of interpreting "transference." She said that "the attitude of most analysts today towards counter-transference is to consider it highly dangerous and to avoid it," though it is "a known and recognized phenomenon."

In her view, Freud's demand that the analyst "recognize" and "master" his countertransference does not lead to the conclusion that countertransference is a disturbing factor and the analyst should become unfeeling and detached "but that he must use his emotional response as a key to the patient's unconscious." This protects the analyst, she explained, from entering as a "co-actor on the scene" that the patient re-enacts in the analytic relationship, and from exploiting the relationship for the analyst's needs. At the same time the analyst will find ample stimulus "for taking himself to task again and again and for continuing the analysis of his own problems."

To her mind, Little says, "it is this question of a paranoid or phobic attitude towards the analyst's own feelings which constitutes the greater danger and difficulty in counter-transference. The very real fear of being flooded with feeling of any kind, rage, anxiety, love, etc., in relation to one's patient and of being passive to it and at its mercy, leads to an unconscious avoidance or denial. Honest recognition of such feeling is essential to the analytic process." She adds that if there is insincerity on the part of the analyst, the patient will respond to it with anger and will also identify with the analyst as a means of denying his own feelings, to the detriment of the analysis. The patient will fail to recognize objectively the irrational parental behavior that has been so powerful a factor in the development of his neurosis, for whenever the analyst behaves like the patient's parents and "conceals the fact he is doing so," the patient represses his original anxiety and rage.

The analyst must allow the patient to grow without either interference or over-stimulation, and this can happen, she says, only insofar as analysis is a true sublimation for the analyst "and not a per-version or addiction (as I think it sometimes may be)." She grants that interpretation of countertransference along lines she indicates "would make much heavier demands on analysts" but adds that so did the interpretation of transference. She notes that the use of transference has been discovered to have compensations in that "the analyst's libidinal impulses and creative reparative wishes find ef-fective gratification in the greater power and success of his work." She adds, "I believe that similar results might follow a greater use of counter-transference if we can find ways of using it."

Langs pays tribute to Heinrich Racker, mentioned before, for the concept of "unconscious collusion." This is a process in which the analyst repeats the patient's traumatic past (by acting like one or both of the parents of childhood), creating the "neurotic vicious circle" Strachey mentioned, not only reinforcing the patient's own pathology but passing on to the patient the analyst's pathology. This concept was borne out by the unconscious perceptions of patients that Langs uncovered.

Racker wrote on "The Meanings and Uses of Counter-trans-ference," in the *Psychoanalytic Quarterly*, 1972. He discussed aspects of countertransference, including interactional pathology — patho-logical transference and countertransference that served to repeat, rather than modify, the pathogenic past of both patient and thera-pist, reinforcing their present pathology.

He cited Dr. Sandor Lorand, who wrote in 1946 of the dangers of countertransference in analytic work, urging that countertransfer-ence reactions be taken into account. Lorand discussed specific prob-lems such as the analyst's conscious desire to heal, the relief analysis may afford the analyst from personal problems, the analyst's nar-cissism and the interference of personal motives in clinical problems. Lorand believed that unless analysts had solved their own conflicts, they could not be of much help to patients.

Racker declared that the lack of "scientific investigation of countertransference must be due to rejection by analysts of their own countertransferences — a rejection that represents unresolved strug-gles with their own primitive anxiety and guilt. . . . We must begin the revision of our feelings about our own countertransferences and try to overcome our own infantile ideals more thoroughly, accepting more fully the fact that we are still children and neurotics even when we are adults and analysts."

He claimed that "whatever the analyst experiences emotionally, his reactions always bear some relation to processes in the patient. Even the most neurotic countertransference ideas arise only in response to certain patients and to certain situations of these patients, and they can, in consequence, indicate something about the patients and their situations."

Langs' interactional approach was influenced by the work of Madeleine Baranger and Willy Baranger. They described the psychoanalytic situation as a "bipersonal field" in 1966 in the chapter, "Insight in the Analytic Situation" for *Psychoanalysis in the Americas*, edited by Dr. Robert E. Litman. It was this concept, Langs says, that first made him realize contributions from both patient and therapist had to be taken into account, especially when ground rules were broken. He believed "the idea of a frame for the bipersonal field was very important—if the frame was there, the field was secure but if the frame was damaged, the field was not secure."

He also began to realize, he said, as reflected in his later writings, that "frame" was too rigid a concept and the "field" concept did not have enough of the communicative quality of the relationship. So he shifted in 1975 to the concept of the "bipersonal field" where there was a spiralling conscious, but especially unconscious, communicative interaction.

In their description of this bipersonal process, the Barangers emphasize the mutuality and interactional aspects of treatment. They note how the analyst's interpretations and selection of material direct the process: "In spite of the 'passivity' of the analyst, he is involved in the patient's fantasy. His unconscious responds to it and *contributes to its emergence and formation.* This fantasy can be defined as 'the dynamic structure (of a pair)' which, at every moment, confers meaning to the bipersonal field."

The analytic "pair" sets the dynamics of the field which depends on shared unconscious experiences and the analyst's interpretations.

Each member of the pair tends to create in the analytic relationship a repetition of his own unresolved neurotic past. Both patient and analyst want to be "rescued" or cured through interpretation: "The insight that is specifically analytic is that process of joint comprehension by the analyst and patient of an unconscious aspect of the field, which consequently leads to a reduction in the pathology of the field, and the rescue of the respective parts involved."

The "field" of the analytic situation is structured by the interaction and communications arising from both centers: the analyst and patient. This material is stratified and includes fantasied interchanges with transference and countertransference components. The field is structured by an unconscious fantasy analogous to those within the individual psyche. The bipersonal unconscious fantasy of the field conditions the appearance of the overt verbal content, and includes a distribution of roles between the analyst and patient that includes the emergence of various impulses, awarenesses of danger, defense mechanisms, reciprocal projections, and parts of the self from each participant.

The Barangers introduced the concept of defenses shared by patient and analyst which they called "bastions." Langs refers to these as "sectors of misalliance." They are a part of the therapeutic interaction that "gets sealed off from the analytic work, based on unconscious collusion between patient and analyst, so that neither gets the chance to work through the conflict analytically."

Within the bipersonal field, insight extends beyond self-discovery and becomes the work of two persons, the Barangers say. Insight is always the result of the cooperation between patient and analyst and appears as a discovery "tinged with surprise." At the moment of insight, the observing egos of both patient and analyst coincide in the interpersonal field. They do not unite but coexist and collaborate, creating a moment of shared analytic work. The patient may occasionally teach something to the analyst. Langs' patients taught him of their unconscious perceptions of the therapist.

Dr. Ralph R. Greenson and Milton Wexler made the distinction between the "real" interaction and the transference neurosis, a distinction Langs does not accept. He believes there is only a single relationship, a *total* relationship that includes both transference and nontransference distortions *and* the truth about the therapist. Greenson and Wexler's work deals with aspects that are not transference. In recognizing errors by the therapist, the authors relate them to the conscious perceptions by the patient, not unconscious perceptions.

Greenson and Wexler wrote of "The Non-transference Relationship in the Psychoanalytic Situation," published in 1969 in the *International Journal of Psycho-Analysis*. They suggest there has been undue focus on the transference, with a relative neglect of the nontransference of "real" interaction that takes place between patient and analyst. The full development and analysis of a transference neurosis (the patient's original neurosis as repeated in the transference) requires the recognition, acknowledgment, clarification and even "nurturing" of the nontransference, or the relatively transference-free reactions between patient and analyst.

These authors state transference may be used by analysts to defend themselves against the impact of the analytic relationship. They maintain that "the whole school of analysts which believes that psychoanalytic treatment consists of 'only interpreting'" is guilty of using transference interpretations as a defense. "Some of them seem to interpret the transference so frequently in the course of an hour because they are afraid of the painful affects that they or their patients might otherwise develop," they say. "Others of this group ignore the patient's correct and painful perceptions and judgments concerning the analyst and remain silent or pick up some interpretable material, no matter how trivial."

Greenson and Wexler point out that the analyst's confirmation of a patient's correct perception in regard to some trait, fault or error in the analyst "helps the patient learn to discriminate between reality and fantasy, something all our patients have difficulty with. It also helps break down the patient's infantile wish for us to be omnipotent and omniscient. Furthermore, it can keep the analyst from falling into the God-like conception of himself that our work makes so easily possible. Acknowledging the correctness of a patient's perceptions or beliefs helps strengthen the patient's healthy capacity for object relations. Finally, an admission of fault or error indicates honesty, a basic and vital component of a 'real relationship'."

The authors conclude: "It is important to keep in mind that our patients know us really far less than we know them. Their beliefs and judgments are based on much less evidence than is available to us. Yet everything we do or say, or don't do or say, from the décor of our office, the magazines in the waiting room, the way we open the door, greet the patient, make interpretations, keep silent, and end the hour, reveals something about our real self, not only our professional self."

Langs says if he were to choose the three most important contributions to the understanding of transference and countertransference, Freud's papers would be first, then the paper by Strachey, and finally the articles of Dr. Harold Searles. Searles, according to Langs, has written with conviction and perception for many years about the analytic situation and the interaction between analyst and patient, "discovering aspects almost totally neglected by other writers."

As early as 1948, when Searles was training to be a psychoanalyst in Washington, D.C., he wrote of psychoanalysis as an interactional process between patient and analyst, speaking of the "therapeutic symbiosis" and the patient's unconscious perception of various characteristics of the analyst. This predated Paula Heimann's important paper of 1949.

When Searles and Langs met in 1979 for the dialogues published in *The Therapeutic Experience and Its Setting*, Searles told Langs of the 1948 paper, which had never been published. After rejections by the *Psychoanalytic Quarterly* and *Psychiatry*, Searles put the article away. Langs now read it and published it in the *International Journal of Psychoanalytic Psychotherapy*, of which he is editor.

He says of this article: "It will have a lasting place in the history of psychoanalysis because it described the intricacies of interaction between patient and therapist as no one had dared to do before. Although Searles' concepts are still not incorporated into classical analytic thinking, the paper is as current today as in 1948, when it was revolutionary. It is remarkable that Searles, when a novice in the field, tackled in depth the issues of the interactional relationship, transference and countertransference, all forbidden territory in 1948."

One of Searles' discoveries was that patients not only wish to destroy or have sexual intimacy with their therapists but also want to "cure" them, as they once wanted to "cure" their parents. Searles says everyone possesses to some degree the wish to cure. He describes this curative wish in "The Patient as Therapist to His Analyst," a chapter in *Tactics and Techniques in Psychoanalytic Therapy, Volume II: Countertransference*, edited by Dr. Peter L. Giovacchini, published in 1975.

Searles discovered that stalemates in treatment, when explored, appeared to show that the analyst was receiving "a kind of therapeutic support" from the patient, that "the analyst is most tenaciously clinging to this very mode of relatedness as being one in which he, the analyst, is receiving therapy from the patient, without the conscious knowledge of either of them."

Patients show, over the course of months and years of treatment, "an interest, a genuine caring, as to whether the analyst himself has been growing and thriving during and as a result of their therapeutic ministrations to him," Searles states.

He believes "the healthy infant-mother symbiosis, which normally provides the foundation for later separation, under tragic circumstances fosters the child's becoming not a truly human individual. He becomes what one might call a symbiotic therapist, whose own ego-wholeness is sacrificed throughout life in a truly selfless devotion, to complementing the ego-incompleteness of the mothering person, and of subsequent persons in his life who, in his unconscious, have the emotional meaning of similarly incomplete mothers. Their ego functioning is dependent upon his being sustainingly a part of them. I suggest, more than anything else, the patient's nascent capacity for love and for the development of mature human responsibility, impels him to perpetuate this mode of relatedness."

Langs quotes Dr. Stanley Olinick as saying that one major unconscious motive for becoming an analyst is a need to work out a relationship with a depressed mother. Like Searles, Langs believes patients unconsciously know when a therapist is seeking therapeutic support. It is an axiom of psychoanalytic theory that the profession one selects indicates an unconscious need.

Thus Langs' theories are based on classical psychoanalytic concepts, some of which he has added to and expanded. He uses his own terms — communicative approach, adaptive context, the listening process, lie therapy and truth therapy. He has selected for further exploration what he considers the most neglected area in psychoanalysis — the clinical. He believes psychoanalysis need not be an "impossible profession," as Freud described it. That it can become "possible" if therapists understand more of their unconscious feelings about patients so those feelings will not adversely affect treatment.

9
CONQUERING
WHAT WE FEAR

I asked Langs what originally drove him to study in depth what he believed the Achilles heel of psychoanalysis—the technique of the therapist.

As always, he replied thoughtfully and directly. "We conquer what we fear," he said. "New discoveries come out of an unconscious need."

"And what was your unconscious need?" (With what joy I asked that question of a psychoanalyst!)

"It had several roots. One was in my adult life and there were no doubt several in childhood. As an adult I had the need to explore in depth the power of the interaction between patient and therapist."

He went on: "My need to focus on what was wrong with the technique of analysis came out of the quality of my own analysis. Winnicott once wrote that every book or article by an analyst is an attempt to finish his analysis. After nine-and-a-half years of analysis, some difficulties appeared in my life that may unconsciously have motivated me in my work. I felt there was a missing link in the relationship between the analyst and myself that I had to discover.

"As part of filling in the missing link, I started self-analysis after reading a chapter by Searles titled 'The Patient as Therapist to His Analyst.' It appeared in a book for which I had written a chapter, 'The Patient's Unconscious Perceptions of the Therapist's Errors'. The editor of the book, Dr. Peter L. Giovacchini had sent me Searles' chapter in galleys, thinking I would enjoy it.

"I had already discovered some patients tried to 'correct' the analyst in his errors and now I learned Searles had extended 'correcting' to 'curing'. Freud had given an intellectualized concept of the therapeutic interaction, with the analytic work almost restricted to the patient free associating and the analyst interpreting. I was finding other dimensions to this interaction, most of them unconscious. One was that at the very times the analyst was consciously trying to be curative, he could be unconsciously hurtful. And while the patient was free associating, he could be trying unconsciously to be curative to the analyst.

"This paper and others opened up to me the nature of the transaction between patient and analyst from the traditional, restrictive one of free association by the patient and interpretation by the analyst to a more complex relationship. A relationship involved in the struggle around ground rules, modes of cure, the establishing of a sense of identity in both patient and analyst and the struggle against madness that existed in each."

In Searles' paper, Langs came across the concept that patients unconsciously want to "cure" the therapist as they had wanted to cure their emotionally disturbed parents. It was then, Langs says, he began to understand the patient's unconscious perception of the analyst.

"I realized every conscious perception had a valid unconscious perception that might be quite different," he explained. "I related this to my dissatisfaction with my own analysis. It had not been just my fantasy—my unconscious perceptions of my analyst had been valid though he ignored them. I had been picking up emotional disturbances in the analyst as well as in myself.

"I realized how angry I had been about his modifying ground rules and the lasting effects on me of these breaks. I envied the patient whose analyst provided a secure set of ground rules, a kind of analyst I never knew.

"I realized that what I came to think of as the 'lie system' of my analysis, the total denial by my analyst that he played any part in triggering my reactions and free associations, failed to cure. Thus I had a strong conscious, as well as unconscious motive for finding out the truth about cure."

All through analytic training, Langs said, it troubled him that his teachers reduced every trauma to what had happened in the past. The emphasis was on genetics—the earlier conflicts within, based on forbidden wishes of childhood and the inner prohibitions against carrying them out. Freud had used the case of little Hans to show the boy was afraid to go out into the street because he believed horses would bite off his penis. He unconsciously feared his father would castrate him because he sexually desired his mother, and displaced this fear on the horses.

Freud concluded nothing in reality threatened the neurotic person, only his own taboo wishes. At first Freud had attributed emotional disturbance to reality because his women patients claimed they had been seduced by their fathers. Then Freud realized this was only the daughter's fantasy and the fantasy had caused the neurosis — the wish to possess the father sexually and fear of punishment for the wish. But had there, in some cases, actually been a seduction, or a subtle, partial one, by the father? Langs was plagued by this question, which, he says, Freud considered but never answered because he denied his own seductive manner with patients.

"Blaming the past alone for a patient's unconscious perceptions of the therapist did not make sense to me," Langs said. "I thought there was something 'hollow' about it, a way of getting rid of the troublesome thoughts of the analyst. Analysts laid everything on transference — the patient's feelings and fantasies about his mother and father and the indignities they had inflicted on him. Heaven forbid this might also be true about the analyst and the indignities he may have inflicted on the patient."

When Langs first started to write, he recalls, "I was not discontent in a major way. Some uneasiness, but really not consciously troubled. The only area of issue was the one I started to write about — the interplay between reality and fantasy. Once I discovered the adaptive context and the stimulus, I tried to sort out how much was the patient's unconscious, real perception of the therapist and how much was distortion."

He says that today "I've really come full circle, in that I was taught that much of what we should concentrate on with the patient was distorted and fantasy-based and now I would say that a patient always and consistently initially reacts to a therapist's intervention with valid unconscious perceptions which may then be exaggerated and sometimes distorted. But the unconscious perceptions of the therapist are always the first step in the psychoanalytic process for the patient."

Langs believes his major contribution is the idea of encoded unconscious communication—the way the patient selectively perceives qualities in the analyst that may be interfering with therapy. The patient's traumatic past influences his perception of the unconscious implication of the therapist's interventions primarily when the therapist breaks a ground rule, which, Langs says, most therapists do in one way or another. The understanding by the therapist of how he may be harming the therapy "is the heart of the future of psychotherapy," according to Langs.

The subject of his first paper was no coincidence. It was titled "Day Residues, Recall Residues, and Dreams—Reality and the Psyche." He had given much thought to the reality that prompted a dream, what Freud called the "day residue." It came out of reality—something the patient had seen or experienced the day before which produced emotions so strong they awakened related memories during sleep, when the censors of the mind weakened. Langs puzzled over this interplay between the reality of the day before and the fantasy at night. He did not believe dreaming was completely an intrapsychic process unrelated to reality. He believed, as Freud did, that something in reality had triggered the dream. He wondered if this did not also apply to the free associations of patients in analysis.

Once he turned to technique, it became somewhat automatic, he says, that he studied the long-neglected listening process. He has written the only book to discuss the process—no other book even has a chapter on it.

It is no accident Langs concentrated on the power of the unconscious fantasy. Dr. Jacob Arlow, a famous psychoanalyst, Langs' supervisor when he trained at the psychoanalytic institute, had written on the meaning of the unconscious fantasy and "fantasy constellations." He impressed Langs with the idea that the conscious material offered by the patient was often derived from a fantasy on a deeper level of consciousness. Arlow taught Langs to look for the unconscious fantasy and the memories clustered around it. The fantasy appeared in encoded or disguised form and the analyst had to undo the disguise.

One day the thought struck Langs that, as in a dream, some stimulus (day residue) might be causing on the unconscious level what the patient talked about in each session. Perhaps the patient's thoughts and memories, like a dream, had to be translated from the language of the conscious to the language of the unconscious *as it applied to the therapist as stimulus.* The *therapist* was the "day residue" of the patient's free associations. What the patient suppressed in relation to hurts experienced at the hands of the therapist would appear in displaced form at the next session and the therapist had to decode those hidden references. In other words, whatever the patient spoke about related not only to his past but also to his unconscious perceptions of the analyst. The patient would react to the analyst, now the most important person in his life (as his mother had once been), more intensely than to anyone in the world outside.

Langs now studied the depths stirred in patients by his interventions and read the reports of therapists he supervised. When he came across a patient saying, for instance, after a therapist had made up a missed session (breaking a ground rule), "My mother always treated me like a baby, she never trusted me to go out alone," Langs wondered if this were an unconscious perception of how the therapist had treated the patient — infantilizing him by offering a makeup session, gratifying a childish need instead of cancelling the hour when necessary. Langs wondered how many therapists did not "listen" correctly to patients. While patients were often consciously unreliable, they were very reliable in the unconscious sense, Langs believed — there is no way of persuading our unconscious to tell a lie, lies stem from the conscious part of the ego and superego.

Langs now realized, he says, how many of his "embedded insights" about his own analyst had not been "heard" or accepted by the analyst. Especially when the analyst broke a ground rule and Langs had been unconsciously protesting. He believed his analyst had neglected the responsibility of a therapist to work over with him what he had been unconsciously communicating to the analyst.

"If the therapist is doing something harmful, who else in the world should know about it and try to rectify it?" he says. "This is part of Freud's heritage — his commitment to truth."

Langs hopes his work makes clear the power of the unconscious mind not only in daily behavior but in every therapeutic experience, where the unconscious minds of both patient and therapist are in constant communication. "What I heard from patients taught me everything I know," he says. "Most important, I realized that both patient and therapist cannot understand their own traumatic pasts outside of the analytic relationship. The way to understand the pathology of your past is the way you understand the pathology that exists in the interaction in therapy. It is the way to the past. The past never comes up except in relation to the therapist."

Langs says he was amazed to discover that therapists were so terrified of the perceptions of themselves by patients. He realized therapists also have strong defenses against facing the unpleasant, disturbing aspects of themselves if they have not accepted them in their personal analyses. Such defenses in therapists were discussed at length by Langs and Searles in dialogues that formed the book *Intrapsychic and Interpersonal Dimensions of Treatment.*

Searles also speaks in this book of his personal analysis with the late Dr. Ernest Hadley of Washington, D.C., calling it a "relatively highly classical analysis." Searles told Langs, "I was enormously grateful to Ernest Hadley for what I had gained from him. It's only been in the last ten or fifteen years that it's more and more evident to me how very much was not done, that I have felt much more conscious of what my analysis did *not* accomplish." He added that he had expressed much gratitude to Hadley over the years.

Langs then commented that most "analysands" — young analysts in training — tend to "consciously overidealize their analyst and their analysis" and that "it takes years of working-through within ourselves to really acknowledge that there were constructive and destructive aspects. That there really was good and bad, if I may use such terms."

Searles described how, when he first started analysis, he would drive to Washington from Rockville, Maryland, for a 7 A.M. hour, "free associate as conscientiously as I knew how, and be told once again how hostile I was. I think he [Hadley] should have been interpreting my *fear* of hostility, because I was terrified of my hostility. I was very afraid I would murder someone. I had been afraid for years I would murder someone."

Searles said Hadley never made an interpretation except within the closing minutes of a session: "He was very stereotyped. It took

me many years to become able to make an interpretation any moment when it was timely to do so, even in the opening moments of
a session. It took me many years to become free from my identifications with some of his more obsessive qualities."

He said Hadley had "worked a great deal on my grandiosity.
He came to call me, ironically, 'God Searles'." This, according to
Langs, would be breaking a ground rule, attacking the patient.

Searles described a number of ways in which Hadley broke
ground rules. He permitted Searles to visit him in the hospital when
he had a minor bladder operation. Searles reported, "He wasn't feeling well, and in the course of my being there he threw back the bed
covers and showed me that he had a catheter in his penis and some
bandages holding it there. Any sexual meaning that he may have had
—exhibitionistic sexual meaning—was very much submerged in his
showing me that he was uncomfortable and in physical distress. I
was put in, and felt myself to be in, a comforting kind of position
toward him, a maternal position, I would say." For a therapist to
show his penis to a patient, even under such circumstances, was a
seductive act.

Hadley also told Searles of his personal life, that he had grown
up on a Kansas farm and, when he was twelve, his father made him
go out into the world to earn his living. Searles said, "Hadley once
confided to me, in a spirit of bitter resignation, that he was working himself to death, he said that clearly. At another time, it wasn't
in response to any such cynical bitterness on his part, but simply
an expression of commendation from me to him about how con-
scientious he was, and how hard he worked, it was sincere. I really
felt I was sincere. I remember his shifting about uncomfortably. He
couldn't stand the—I think it was—real expression of positive appreciation of him, but at least he made it possible for me to say it
to him."

Another way Hadley broke ground rules was letting Searles run
up a bill for $3,600, which he paid off in a year. Still another break
occurred when Hadley accepted gifts. Searles recalled, "Ernest had
told me that he felt deficient in his knowledge of art so at my final
session I brought the nicest art book I knew of, *A Treasury of Art
Masterpieces,* edited by Thomas Craven." Also toward the end of
his analysis, Searles noticed that on a table near his elbow as he lay

on the couch stood a set of small china horses. He knew Hadley loved horses and he guessed the replicas had been the gifts of patients who had completed their analyses. He bought Hadley a ceramic bull, larger than any of the horses.

Searles told Langs the "strongest emotion" he felt during analysis was "a murderous feeling *toward my father*" that had always been largely repressed, and that he was eventually able to experience other strong feelings, though the murderous feeling for his father "was the most intense one."

He commented, "My old man's impact on me was absolutely appalling, absolutely indelible, terrible." He described his father, who owned a men's clothing store in Hancock, New York, then a village of 1,500 in the Catskill Mountains, as "a many-sided man, a very diverse man, a man with a marvelous sense of humor, an inexhaustible fund of stories, including dirty jokes, on the other hand a paranoid, bitter, hateful man, a frightening man, a man of latent violence. A male chauvinist pig to the *n*th degree. There was much of this Archie Bunker about him." He said his father, at least once and sometimes twice each night, woke "bellowing with a mixture of terror and rage from a nightmare." His father wanted him to be a doctor, telling him if he went to Johns Hopkins, then Vienna, "You'll have the world by the balls."

Searles describes his mother as born in an even tinier town than Hancock, "a hamlet across the Delaware River in northern Pennsylvania." She was "a handsome woman . . . a schizoid-character kind of person." He recalled her as of a "phallic nature" and subjecting him to "many enemas." Both parents liked to play bridge. He played football and tennis and "loved to dance."

Searles also told Langs that some of Searles' patients called him "coldly sadistic and impersonal and intensely inhospitable." He commented, "So I have to say that there are limits on my ability to help a person come to know his feelings. I think this happens in treatment and maybe if the treatment with these patients goes on long enough, I can come back to this. It's not only that the patient becomes more and more able to face strong feelings but that the analyst, through his experience with that patient, becomes better and better able to face them also."

During the dialogues Searles said that sometimes, if a patient was mute and resistant for months, he would say something personal to the patient. He gave as example: "Several months ago I confided to a middle-aged female that she was, and long had been, my favorite patient. I told her this because I knew that this phenomenon, although in various ways pleasant to me, must indicate one of her major problems. My sharing with her this information (information which represents, obviously, an alteration in my customary participant-observer functioning with my patients collectively) had highly constructive results in terms of the emergence of a wealth of newly remembered transference material.

"She recalled, with intense feelings of murderous rage and grief, how all her life she had felt it absolutely necessary to be pleasing to other people generally and, above all, to her mother. Her negative mother-transference feelings toward me, largely repressed for years in our work, now emerged with an intensity which I found at times frightening and awesome. With all this, she began manifesting a coherence and a purposefulness in her ego-functioning which had been largely lacking before."

Langs called this a modification in ground rules, saying, "You modified both your neutrality and anonymity." Searles replied that the patient, still in treatment, showed an improved level of ego integration and that he regarded his intervention and its aftermath as among the "most durably favorable turning points in my work with her thus far."

Langs told Searles that he was convinced maintaining a stable and secure set of boundaries was vital to establishing what Searles alluded to as "an optimal holding environment." Searles had earlier pointed out that for the psychotic patient who is mute and in the early autistic phase, the maintenance of that hold is the analyst's basic task.

Searles then commented, "You're not forgetting that the patient becomes one's *own* optimal holding environment?"

Langs replied, "No. That's the other side of the holding functions of the ground rules. Dr. Judith Kestenberg, in 1975, writing on infants and mothers and holding, discussed how the infant holds the mother and related it in a general way to the analysand and his analyst. She wrote, too, of how the infant may facilitate being held."

He added that he thought the observing of the ground rules offered "the optimal hold for both patient and analyst or therapist," what Searles called "a therapeutic symbiosis." As soon as a therapist modified the rules, "there is an inherent invitation" toward a pathological symbiosis. Every alteration in a ground rule is a repetition of some meaningful piece of pathological interaction from the past and the deviations confirm the patient's neurosis so that it can't be truly modified verbally."

Searles said he thought "an individual patient's psychopathology is a part of an interpersonal process wherein the psychopathology is mutual in some disguised way."

He praised Langs for his "appreciation of the creativity of patients, their providing unconscious supervision to the therapist, their providing the material needed for him to make interpretations." To which Langs replied, "Much of that was inspired by your papers. Once you put me on the beam, I think I did some valid things with it. But I have no idea how long it would have taken me without your contributions."

Searles then referred to a passage by Langs in *The Bipersonal Field* that he found "very helpful." The passage read: "We see here something that is absolutely characteristic of both the patient and the therapist, although hopefully it will be in different proportions for each. There is the wish to cure and be cured, and there is the wish to remain ill and do harm. In fact, even in the patient's or therapist's most destructive communications and hurtful interactional efforts, there is a kernel of therapeutic intention and hope." Searles added, "In my work with patients I suffered a great deal from a fear that I am basically, when all the rest is said and done, diabolical. And I found this passage in your book very helpful."

He called this book "the most major contribution to psychoanalysis I have ever encountered toward an integration of what you call the interpersonal dimension into classical psychoanalytic theory and technique."

He commented, "I've learned a great deal from this book and have devoted more time to it than to any other I've read in years." He praised particularly Langs' statement that "the therapist's appropriate love is expressed by maintaining the boundaries" and for indicating that "further appropriate expression of love would be an accurate and well-timed interpretation."

Searles said that since reading *The Bipersonal Field* he found his work with patients "to be going differently." He mentioned a chronically schizophrenic patient who had been "talking voluminously, as she often does," and said he had interjected a comment he thought deserved to be called to her attention "before the material would become stale for her, as it had in the past."

He reported, "She looked a bit interrupted for only a moment, and went on with, seemingly, hardly a pause or change in her course. But then, within at most two minutes later, I heard, in the midst of her voluminous talking (highly delusional as usual) her describing how someone—a fellow patient, so I gathered—had thrown some explosive material into the television set. This was clearly delusional in content, but I felt sure it had to do with my having thrown in, as it were, that comment only a couple of minutes before. This delusion of hers involved not simply the projection of something entirely intrapsychic on her part, but sprang in part from an interpersonal contribution from me—that is, the comment I had thrown in."

Langs, returning the compliment, mentioned Searles' paper on how a patient's symptoms may serve as a transitional object for the analyst just before termination of treatment. Langs said, "There you very perceptively tune in on the analyst's investment in the patient's pathology. That is another very important subject, because the prevailing idealized model of the analyst is, of course, that he wants only to help the patient to get rid of that pathology. Few have acknowledged the investment that the analyst has in sustaining such pathology."

Searles commented, "Your way of putting it gets me to thinking that it's a relatively commonplace concept for analysts to be aware that the patient's loss of symptoms is a loss, isn't it?"

Then he added, "That's not earthshakingly new, that analysts realize the change for the patient is going to involve loss. So, it seems to me, the analyst's coming to develop a very considerable conscious emotional investment in the patient's symptoms is all part and parcel of that, in order that *he* will know at first hand something of the *patient's* loss in changing for the better."

Langs replied, "Still, I think analysts very much deny the extent to which they miss the terminated patient and experience his loss — though such emotions should be kept within limits. And I think one of the ways in which analysts have maintained their denial of meaningful loss is through very frequent modifications in the ground rules during the period of termination. Unfortunately, that tends to modify the opportunity for the patient to work through the separation experience. It also softens the trauma for the analyst, by providing him a last moment of pathological symbiosis."

Langs said he thought it a myth that the termination phase rounds out the patient's "erratic course toward health." He explained he thought the termination phase introduced "a new set of anxieties and problems and a new regression in every patient and in the analyst."

The dialogue between these two men shows how they have pioneered in the understanding of the interaction between patient and therapist. Each set off to explore a difficult psychic frontier and neither has been very heartily accepted by the psychoanalytic community. Each has strong adherents, yet also many critics.

But they are two who have dared, as Langs expresses it, "to conquer what we fear."

10
CRITICS AND
ADMIRERS

Langs is a controversial figure in psychoanalytic circles. There are prominent analysts who comment, "He has some important things to say but . . . " and launch into such remarks as "He is too dogmatic," "He has an abrasive manner," "He is grandiose in his presentation," "He should have had another analysis instead of writing all those books."

There has also been praise. Dr. Rebecca Z. Solomon, past president of the American Psychoanalytic Association, in her review of *The Technique of Psychoanalytic Psychotherapy* which appeared in the *American Journal of Psychiatry,* September, 1974, said: "At times Dr. Langs' conclusions may appear arbitrary and simplistic, but his overall approach is sensitive, comprehensive and thoughtful. This book is a welcome addition to the literature and can be useful to the practitioner and supervisor of psychotherapy."

The overall reviews of Langs' fifteen books show a wide variance in regard to critical opinion. Sometimes one reviewer will be both highly critical and praiseworthy. Dr. Merton Gill in reviewing *The Therapeutic Environment* for *Contemporary Psychology* in 1981 (Volume 26, No. 1) said: "Taking the Freudian view of human psychology essentially for granted, Langs concerns himself with therapeutic technique. I consider his views a major step forward. Essentially, he attempts to integrate the interpersonal and intrapsychic points of view in technique. . . . Langs is by no means the only one who attempts such an integration. But he comes from the Freudian side, and his attempt is so systematic, explicit, and thoroughgoing that it is indeed something new under the sun. Langs deserves a full measure of thanks for his work on an integration that is absolutely essential for progress in the field."

Gill says the technique Langs describes is applicable to both psychoanalysis and psychotherapy. He explains: "That statement does not mean that *psychoanalysis* and *psychotherapy,* as those terms are currently defined by most people, *are* conducted by the same technique. It means rather that the technique he advocates *can* and should be used not only in the optimal circumstances for psychoanalysis but even in a less than optimal frame (that is, even with lesser frequency, even with chair rather than couch) with sicker patients, and by less experienced therapists."

Gill also had criticisms. He maintained that Langs "takes an absolutist rather than relativist view of the real and the unreal. He incorrectly assumes it is possible for a therapist to distinguish sharply between the two." Gill suggests patient and therapist "should work with the understanding that multiple views of reality are possible."

His second criticism is that Langs places great stress on the validation of interpretation. "He is right to do so, and he is right to recognize that *implications* in the manifest associations are important clues to the patient's response to the interventions and hence to whether an interpretation was 'correct' or not," Gill says. "But again, not only is he dichotomous to too great a degree about correct and incorrect, but he also too readily forgets that implications are inferences and that inferences may be mistaken. He does not recognize . . . that validation is a complex and arduous matter, and that he is wrong to imply that his work is validated research."

He said however that Langs' work shows "the power of the recognition that therapy is indeed an interpersonal matter in which the patient's experience of the relationship is significantly contributed to by the therapist's behavior," and also "how little this is recognized and taught."

He sums up: "Langs has shot to prominence like a meteor. He threatens to become a cult, and has embarked on a series of seminars in various cities to carry the message. His increasingly expanding set of new terms has developed to the point that he now includes a glossary in his books. His success at once has riled the establishment and delighted — and I insist instructed — many. He writes prolifically, repetitively, and with an unmistakable air of self-congratulation.

He outrages many by converting tape recordings of his supervisory teaching into books. It would be a pity if these matters of promotion of his ideas led to their having a fate like that of a meteor. But even if that should happen, I am convinced that the core ideas are sound and important. They are that the patient's experience of the relationship is contributed to by the therapist as well as the patient, that this experience is frequently only alluded to in the patient's associations, and that the analysis of this experience is the first step in the analysis of the transference, the central feature of psychoanalytic technique."

A careful, impartial reading of Langs' *The Listening Process* "is hardly likely to leave any therapist indifferent or unchanged. Aside from the book being a treasure trove of scintillating ideas and thought-provoking concepts and theories, it also challenges the reader to compare and evaluate his own ways of doing therapy with the rigorous, exacting standards of the author," wrote Dr. Marvin P. Osman, of Beverly Hills, in the *Journal of the American Academy of Psychoanalysis,* 1981 (Volume 9, No. 2).

Osman said that though Langs regards his thinking as founded entirely on "classical psychoanalytic theory," he undoubtedly "should be included among those analytic investigators who are truly creative and independent and have no compunction in differing from traditional psychoanalysts or their viewpoints."

However, there are instances, Osman adds, where "an overly strict and rigid maintenance of the frame could represent a dehumanized, mechanical stance or be a cover for unconscious sadism. . . . There is no substitute for utilizing one's clinical judgment tailored to a particular situation. One should bear in mind that sins of omission could be even greater under certain circumstances than the sins of commission. . . . This is for each therapist to evaluate in the light of his personal experience and in conjunction with the particular clinical problem."

In 1980, in the *International Review of Psycho-Analysis* Patrick J. Casement, a member of the British Society of Psycho-Analysis, praised *The Therapeutic Environment* as offering "much to teach even the most experienced analysts." He said, "To read it nondefensively is to be shriven but also to be enriched. It has much to offer anyone open to new ideas, and willing to learn, and in our practice as therapists and analysts who amongst us can afford to be otherwise?"

Dr. Merl M. Jackel, a New York psychoanalyst, reviewing *The Bipersonal Field* in the *International Journal of Psycho-Analysis,* wrote, "For the young therapist or aspiring analyst, this book brings out more clearly than any book I have read the importance of the framework; the need to carefully assess the patient's associations for realistic perceptions of the analyst as well as transference elements; the advisability of a personal analysis; and the continuing need for self-observation and self-analysis. For this reviewer, it clarified some post-Kleinian concepts. It contains many astute and valuable clinical observations."

He pointed out, however, that in the reported seminars the therapists were all young paraprofessionals beginning their training, inexperienced and analytically naive. . . . As a result gross errors in technique were frequent and repetitive, creating chaotic therapeutic situations. This makes scientific evaluation of the interactions problematical. . . . In Langs' own terms, the field was a grossly pathological one. . . . all patients were treated in a hospital clinic. . . . In such a setting, the one-to-one relationship, the anonymity of the analyst, the maintenance of confidentiality, the atmosphere of timelessness are difficult, if not impossible, to maintain." Jackel concluded by saying, "One would hope that Langs will write another similar book using for material his own analytic cases." This, Langs will not do, for, as he says, he does not use his patients, early discovering they recognized themselves in the pages of his books and confidentiality went down the drain.

Dr. W. W. Meissner, in the *International Journal of Psycho-Analysis,* 1978 (Volume 59), called Langs' two volumes, *The Technique of Psychoanalytic Psychotherapy,* "a significant and valuable contribution to the literature on psychotherapy as based on and derived from psychoanalytic principles." He says the work is intended as an introductory treatise and therefore of value to those starting the study of psychoanalytic psychotherapy and for those continuing to perfect their knowledge and grasp of psychoanalytic principles in applying them to psychotherapeutic contexts.

"The primary value of Langs' work is that it provides a clear, comprehensive, systematic and theoretically consistent approach to the application of psychoanalytic principles in psychotherapy," Meissner writes. "There have been few sources to which the psychotherapy supervisor could refer his students prior to this that offer anywhere near the comprehensiveness and systematic presentation of analytic ideas for the psychotherapist as these volumes. But even more experienced clinicians may find Langs' clear, concise, and often illuminating discussions helpful in putting principles of psychoanalytic psychotherapy in perspective."

After explaining in detail the contents of the books and their theories, he praises Langs' "clarity and directness of expression which is admirably maintained throughout." Then he raises two points of criticism. The first is that there is little sense of diagnostic discrimination, that Langs "writes as though one could presume that all patients fell into more or less the same category and that what he was describing or attempting to teach was a universally applicable therapeutic modality." In the practice of analysis, Meissner says, diagnostic discriminations are of the utmost importance, particularly in the assessment of analyzability but also in the determination of what kinds of treatment are appropriate for particular patients. Diagnostic discriminations are important even in a more refined way from moment to moment of the therapeutic encounter, in connection with what kind of technical interventions are called for, to what degree, with what level of interpretation and with what dosage. Meissner asserts, "All these judgments which Langs so beautifully develops in his discussions of them are ultimately controlled by diagnostic considerations."

He explains further: "One does not get from Langs' account a good sense of the modifications of therapeutic approach and the differentiation in technical implementation of the therapy that would take place between, let us say, a neurotic hysterical patient and a more primitive narcissistic borderline. Greater diagnostic sensitivity, therefore, it would seem to me, would be of great assistance in the more flexible adaptation of therapeutic means to specific therapeutic goals for specific patients and for specific forms of psychopathology."

His second criticism is that Langs writes as an analyst who brings to the psychotherapeutic situation the resources of his analytic experience and skill and, consequently, the reader does not gain a sense of how the psychotherapist goes about working with resistances and interpretations or dealing with transference and countertransference in a way that differs in any significant degree from what might be experienced in the analytic context.

Meissner concludes that despite the shortcomings, "I would like to emphasize . . . that these volumes form a unique contribution to the literature on psychoanalytic psychotherapy. . . . I know of no other volumes which have achieved an equivalent level of sophistication, consistency, clarity and thoroughness of presentation. . . . They can be warmly recommended as a substantial contribution to this growing and important literature."

Dr. Victor Calef of San Francisco, reviewing *The Bipersonal Field* for the *Journal of the American Psychoanalytic Association* in 1979, Volume 27, had several criticisms of Langs' theories. He said Langs' "emphasis and ardor (critical zeal?) become, in my view, depreciating of his students." He criticized Langs' "attempts to show the identity of psychotherapy and psychoanalysis while maintaining their differences, as if his concepts resolve all the difficulties as well as the paradoxes of 'psychoanalytic psychotherapy'."

He suggests there may be "an interesting confessional thread in Langs' lectures" in that he "recognizes his loquaciousness, which he compares with the succinct communications from patients. He defends himself against his potential critics by saying they will say he has gone crazy. The purposes of such protective devices are clear but unnecessary.

"Langs writes as the keeper of the faith, as a voice in the wilderness among the few who wish to keep the analytic situation intact and safe from encroachment. For this reader, the application of psychoanalysis, the sermons, and the methods advocated in this volume represent misuse, even abuse, of observation and theory. The language tends to be jingoistic, while conjectures and claims are extravagant. Aspiring to be both critic and exponent of psychoanalysis, Langs falls short in both attempts. Moreover, the violations of basic educational principles that Langs permits himself are, to say the least, regrettable."

Dr. Robert T. Fintzy in 1978, reviewing *The Listening Process* in the *Southern California Psychiatric Society News* attacked the book as far too long and for its "merciless criticism of each and every presenter [of cases]," saying, "One has to be a truly compulsive reader like myself to persevere through the entirety of this (mono) tone."

But the first sentence of his review reads, "Once again, Robert Langs has many interesting and creative ideas to present." He also praises "the valuable part of this book, the Appendix, which capsulizes the many, many views he has about the therapeutic experience, views which expand upon his previous insights."

The following year Fintzy reviewed *The Therapeutic Interaction,* saying, "More than any other book in my memory, this one vibrantly depicts how very much of the essence and being of the analyst is actively involved in the therapeutic interaction. We are reminded that the analytic setting can present *both* participants, not just the patient, with multiple opportunities for bilateral therapeutic regression and misalliances. *Shared* interactional blind spots frequently can cause pathology of the bipersonal field. Thus, it is essential for the analyst to know his own personal equation, acknowledge his own *inevitable* inner difficulties, silently modify such and then refocus on the patient." He concluded his review: "Langs is an erudite, articulate, creative thinker, and this book reflects such."

There are classical psychoanalysts who essentially agree with Langs but claim he asks too much of the therapist. When Langs wrote "The Therapeutic Relationship and Deviations in Technique," an article he first submitted to Dr. Joseph Sandler of London, then editor of the *International Journal of Psycho-Analysis,* Sandler returned the article with the comment, "Unfortunately, we are unable to accept this. You are asking too much of the analyst."

Langs says of this rejection, "There was nothing analysts could refute in what I said except that I was 'asking too much'. *I'm* not asking too much. They mean the *patient* is asking too much. But it isn't too much. It's what the patient is entitled to."

He continues, "Patients deserve the best we can give them. To those who say I am asking too much of analysts, I ask, 'What is too much?' That they know their own unconscious feelings and thoughts, as they are asking the patient to know his? I mean really *'know.'* Not intellectually but emotionally. Through ongoing self-analysis. As Freud suggested."

Langs' article, "Modes of 'Cure' in Psychoanalysis and Psychoanalytic Psychotherapy" was accepted by the *International Journal of Psycho-Analysis* in 1981, when Thomas T. S. Hayley became editor. After the article appeared in the *Journal* (Volume 62, Part 2), it drew a critical letter from Gertrude Blanck and Rubin Blanck of New York City, published in the next issue of the *Journal* in 1982 (Volume 63, Part 1).

In this letter the Blancks asserted they had engaged in personal communication with Langs informing him that he was misrepresenting their position in this paper and "that he chose to proceed with publication nevertheless is clear indication that this misrepresentation is intentional."

They stated: "In his paper Dr. Langs uses material from a case contributed by one of our students as a 'vignette that helps us characterize manifest listening and intervening (p. 202).' The original material in our book, *Ego Psychology: Theory and Practice,* pages 305–306, was presented line-by-line in order to offer the reader an opportunity to follow as closely as possible exactly what transpired between patient and therapist. We had no way of conveying what went on in the therapist's mind, but we have no doubt that there was due consideration for unconscious communication. Dr. Langs' version paraphrases this material, thus enabling him to slant it to his own purposes. Thus, he is able to conclude that 'there is no concept of an unconscious communicative interplay between patient and therapist' (p. 202).

"In fact, the very thrust of Dr. Langs' paper is to prove that very few analysts other than he understand and use the concept of unconscious communication. There is no way to accomplish such a purpose other than to distort the positions of other analysts for, by definition, every analyst uses unconscious communication as a concept every day in every case that he or she treats. Perhaps the style of usage is not to Dr. Langs' liking, but that is another matter.

"If Dr. Langs does indeed have a valid point to make, surely it can stand on its own merits without requiring that he misrepresent the views of others for the questionable advantage of placing himself in a better light. We informed him that, when we summarized the works of the ego psychologists, we showed them the manuscript before publication in order to ensure that we were representing them correctly. We suggested that we are available for Dr. Langs to follow this method with us. Obviously, he has chosen not to do so.

"The other living authors to whom Dr. Langs refers can, we are sure, defend themselves. Those who knew the late Dr. Ralph R. Greenson may speculate about the searing comments he would have made in his defense."

The following issue of the *Journal* contained a letter Langs wrote in October 1981 replying to the Blancks' charges. He said he had hoped his paper on modes of cure, which took issue with important segments of present day psychoanalytic listening and formulating, would "spark much needed thought and clinical debate" and that discussion would be "basically empirical, definitive, and specific, rather than personal and with efforts to malign my character and intentions."

He added that some years ago, when he began his extensive studies of the listening process and therapeutic interaction, he, too, assumed, "as the Blancks do," that every analyst made consistent use of the concept of unconscious communication between the patient and analyst in daily work. He stated:

"A study of the psychoanalytic literature, however, including the work of these two authors, proved empirically that such an assumption is unfortunately quite unfounded. I discovered as well in many psychoanalysts—including the Blancks—an apparent split between their theoretical thinking and beliefs, and their actual clinical efforts. It was observations of this kind that prompted the particular paper under discussion."

He said his article was the result of an extensive body of writings in which he made use of his own clinical and supervisory observations to document his formulations. He called the article an attempt to re-examine aspects of psychoanalytic technique in light of the findings he developed through clinical investigations. The effort by the Blancks "to question my motives and capacities as a clinical observer and reader ignores this work and the dedication to psychoanalysis reflected therein. It cannot serve the field of psychoanalysis to attempt to dismiss new and serious findings without comprehending their scientific basis and responding accordingly.

"As for the ill-defined complaint that I have slanted the Blancks' material and distorted their position, a rereading of their vignette reveals once again an entirely manifest content approach devoid of consideration of encoded or derivative expression, and therefore of any attention to the ongoing communicative (conscious and) unconscious interaction between patient and therapist. I found no evidence of misrepresentation, nor do the Blancks offer any specific data to refute my observations. Their additional comments have no bearing on the scientific and technical issues involved, and I will not dignify them with further response."

He then took up "the unfortunate allusion to Ralph Greenson, who was a dear friend and colleague." He said, "Greenson knew of my work and encouraged it without reservation. Committed to the pursuit of psychoanalytic truths and to the growth of psychoanalysis through clinically founded extensions and revision, he was prepared to rethink his own position in the light of my own observations. Greenson was in fact marvelously open to my ideas and their challenge. He himself had written of the unfortunate fate of new ideas in psychoanalysis, decrying the extent to which psychoanalysts tend to dismiss in off-hand fashion concepts that threaten their fixed thinking and equilibrium. He detailed the manner in which many important unique findings and ideas were extruded from, rather than integrated into, the main body of psychoanalytic thinking and practice. Such attitudes are still in evidence, though perhaps (or hopefully) less so than when Greenson called this issue to our attention."

He concluded: "Psychoanalysis can maintain its vitality and clinical pertinence only if psychoanalysts themselves discover and define the inevitable flaws in both their theory and practice, and are prepared to change accordingly. However, this is possible only if we put aside personal prejudice and investigate differences in clinical thinking on the basis of psychoanalytically validated clinical observations. Every dedicated psychoanalytic writer must indeed accept such challenges since they offer critical opportunities for fresh understanding and growth. I for one have always welcomed such discussions and will continue to do so."

Therapists who do not understand Freud and who practice only the superficial, fad therapies have also castigated Langs. Some wrote angry letters to the *Los Angeles Times* in response to a column by Langs on May 26, 1982, about the John Hinckley Jr. case. The headline read:

'FEEL GOOD' PSYCHOTHERAPY ON TRIAL
Testimony in Hinckley Case
Shows Danger in the Technique

Langs started off with the charge that "the psychiatric testimony regarding John Hinckley Jr. has placed therapy itself on trial." He was referring not to the clashing points of view as to whether Hinckley was "sane" or "insane," offered by the prosecution and defense psychiatrists, but to the "pained testimony" of Dr. John H. Hopper Jr., the psychiatrist who treated Hinckley before he tried to assassinate President Reagan.

Langs said Hopper's testimony had evoked both "compassion and criticism." The latter centered on Hopper's "admittedly inadequate evaluation of Hinckley's illness and his use of surface-oriented family and behavior therapy techniques." Langs added that "a deeper assessment and treatment procedure, perhaps on an individual basis, might have proved more revealing and helpful."

As though bearing Langs out, three of the men struck by bullets in Hinckley's attack — James S. Brady, the President's press secretary, Timothy J. McCarthy, a Secret Service agent, and Thomas Delahanty, a police officer in Washington, D.C., where the shooting took place on March 30, 1981 — have sued Dr. Hopper for $14,000,000. The suit was announced in Denver on March 18, 1983, in an Associated Press story carried around the world.

The lawsuit accused the psychiatrist of negligence and misdiagnosis, claiming that Dr. Hopper made Hinckley's mental condition worse and failed to heed signals by his patient that he might attempt a political assassination. Brady, who suffered brain damage, sued for $8 million; McCarthy, who suffered lung and liver damage, $2 million; and Delahanty, wounded in the neck by a bullet, $4 million. A Denver judge threw the suit out of court.

As Meissner pointed out, Langs has been criticized for not allowing for "a sense of diagnosis," for presuming all patients fall into the same category, not distinguishing between the "normal neurotic," "borderline" and "psychotic." Analytic theory stresses that what is pathological is a consequence of unconscious conflicts. There are analysts who believe any degree of illness can be treated by psychoanalytic psychotherapy but others who think severe pathology can be treated chiefly by medication because *ego strength* is lacking and the person cannot accept interpretations of his conflicts.

A second criticism is that Langs speaks of psychoanalysis and psychotherapy as though they were the same, not distinguishing what may be appropriate technique to one but not the other. A number of therapists believe the theory and technique of psychoanalysis are valid and applicable to both psychoanalysis and psychoanalytic therapy. They maintain that because the patient goes five times a week and lies on the couch does not necessarily assure that analysis is taking place. Whereas a patient may be in psychoanalytic therapy once or twice a week, sitting up and facing the analyst, and "the process may be analytic — what makes treatment analytic is how the patient behaves and how the therapist behaves," as one analyst puts it.

Langs has also been criticized for claiming to be the only therapist who "listens" to patients. He replies to these critics, "Many analysts believe they know the patient's unconscious communication, claiming my work adds nothing new. They call me radical when I say there *is* something new in technique, that technique cannot be carried on without the unconscious of the analyst influencing the patient's behavior and free associations. Those who claim I have not discovered anything new do not understand what I am saying. They are unable to visualize the concept of interpreting treatment on the basis of the interaction of patient and therapist on the unconscious level."

Some critics accuse him of moralizing, of being too rigid about the ground rules. He says, "I think this is a distortion based on my frank discussion of issues I feel damaging to patients. Many analysts deviate subtly, not grossly, without realizing what they do. They sign insurance forms. They indulge in some revelation about a patient to a colleague or a relative of the patient. They use their homes as offices. They change the patient's hour. They raise fees. And, while I've emphasized the hurtful part, I have also said these breaks can be insightful experiences for both patient and analyst if properly handled and analyzed."

One critic calls Langs' work "invaluable" then criticizes him for being "too perfectionistic." Another critic charges that Langs "appears to need to control the situation . . . is not analytic enough in his supervision . . . is too inflexible," in contrast to a reviewer who calls Langs "very flexible and open to change."

A book reviewer castigates Langs for attacking the therapist because he makes a mistake and another reviewer asserts Langs does not attack therapists for making a mistake but for not recognizing the importance of the error in its effect on the therapeutic relationship.

At the annual midwinter meeting of the American Psychoanalytic Association at the Waldorf Astoria in December 1982, Dr. Stanley J. Coen of New York spoke on "The Analyst's Uses and Misuses of Clinical Theory: Interpretation." The program notes summarizing his speech read:

"The author argues for further consideration of the psychology of the analyst's belief in and use of clinical psychoanalytic theory. The analyst's own subjective distress in the psychoanalytic situation, when this must be hidden from the analyst's introspection, especially with patients with more severe preoedipal psychopathology, leads to defensive misuse of clinical theory. Examples of how theory may be misused defensively by the analyst are drawn from the concept of the analyst as a new object for the patient; this tends to interfere with the analysand's further individuation.

"The rigidity of an analyst's clinical theory, whether oedipal or preoedipal, positivist or subjectivist, exclusively focused on the patient or on the psychoanalytic dialogue, reflects the analyst's own anxiety and insecurity and the need for dogmatic belief in and idealization of his theory. The analyst's own subjective distress causes him to move beyond interpretation, beyond transference, into biology, appeal to the authority of other disciplines, to mechanistic models, and to extra-analytic interventions."

A number of analysts believe what Langs is saying adds to clinical theory. Dr. Walter A. Stewart, former member of the faculty of the New York Psychoanalytic Institute, thinks Langs "has focused emphasis on an issue that has been ignored. His work has a pioneer quality. It is a systematic study of an extremely important point — the interaction that exists between therapist and patient. It is useful to psychoanalysis."

But Langs feels on the whole that his reception by the classical psychoanalysts has been cool. He compares himself to the messenger who brings bad news and must be killed. The leading psychoanalytic journals for the most part, with the exception of the *International Journal of Psycho-Analysis,* have refused to publish his articles, dismiss them as offering nothing new.

He says rejections make him feel depressed, that he realizes he still has "an inappropriate need for the approval of my colleagues, for their sanction, for their love — one of the conscious motives for my work. Some of this has to do with my need to belong and with wanting to prove I was worth accepting as a candidate."

His discoveries, he says, "came out of dogged observations and a determination to discover the truth and be rid of restrictive prejudices. A 'let the chips fall where they may' approach. There is also a positive side to alienation and having to validate observations that threaten other analysts and are rejected out of hand by them. You become your own person, freer to observe and follow a given line of thought, and you sharpen your validation."

He adds, "This is not martyrdom or masochism but a love of truth. A dedication to fathom the truth regardless of personal cost. An obligation and responsibility to patients that cannot, in good conscience, be otherwise.

"I believe in following the love of truth in the face of pain, the necessary pain that goes with discovery of new ideas. I think this is where much of the opposition comes from. New ideas frighten many analysts and impinge upon areas and counter transference-based gratifications and defenses they find too difficult to confront and modify—resolve."

He is convinced clinical creativity in analysis challenges the unresolved countertransferences shared by the group, "ones that confront us, in a sense, with our own madness. Racker wrote of how analysts can pass on to their analysands their own blind spots, their countertransferences. It is an obvious point but one whose implications tend to be ignored. There is a kind of massive sharing, it's like the Emperor's new clothes—a great need to conform even when you sense something is awry."

He muses, "It has been my lot for better or worse to be the innocent child who sees the truth, but I never saw it as a choice. As physician and psychoanalyst, once I found a method of listening and validating, I had no choice but to follow through. Wherever it would take me."

It has taken him into some stormy psychic waters. But he would never dream of avoiding them if he believed that by sailing in he could provide a more effective way of helping ease the distress of the patient.

11
THE STUDENTS
SPEAK

A psychologist from the Midwest, who has been practicing psychotherapy for twenty-two years, working first in social agencies, then for the past fifteen years in private practice, was talking about his recent training with Langs.

He said, "In the past, somehow intuitively, I began to understand there were some things very wrong with therapy. I started to wonder who was really sick—patient or therapist? I deplored the therapeutic 'fast food' mentality of our times which says, 'Make me feel good *now*, no matter the cause of my unhappiness'. Therapies that obliged were like pushers to junkies. A yardstick of symptom removal was used as criterion for 'cure'. I thought, 'We have a fragmented society, we're settling for scraps from the therapeutic table'."

One day he picked up *The Bipersonal Field* and was fascinated. He went to Pittsburgh to hear Langs conduct a one-day workshop. He began tape supervision with Langs, then telephone supervision. It changed his whole approach to therapy. He realized how superficial his prior work had been. He says, "I am very grateful to Dr. Langs. He is brilliant not only in how quickly he picks up the listening process but also in understanding the patient's deeper conflicts. He is a sensitive man who helps in a non-possessive way."

This psychologist is one of the increasing number of Langs' students. The need to teach is strong in Langs, another area in which he uses his whirlwind energy. He founded and is director of the Society for Psychoanalytic Psychotherapy, approaching three hundred members and growing steadily. It sponsors the psychotherapy training program at Lenox Hill Hospital in New York, part of the Division of Psychiatry which is in the Department of Medicine.

The Society also sponsors the *International Journal of Psychoanalytic Psychotherapy*, of which Langs has been editor since 1971.

Most of the articles are written by classical analysts but Langs will publish any paper he believes of merit. Dr. Joel Paris, a psychiatrist, recently wrote Langs to thank him for publishing an article with whose theme Langs disagrees. Paris maintains patients suffered no detrimental consequences as a result of "no fee" psychotherapy as it exists under health insurance in Canada and Great Britain. Langs is particularly open to papers with new ideas because of the hostility he has encountered in many editors and editorial boards of the established journals.

The first annual meeting of the Society was held in October 1982, at Lenox Hill Hospital, and Langs invited me to attend. Featured speakers were to be Searles and Langs. The event was highlighted in advance in the Society's *Newsletter*, edited by Aphrodite Clamar, a psychologist. It reported that registration (which included a psychologist, Kirsten Artin, from Malmo, Sweden) was high.

A short article in the *Newsletter*, "Conflict Theory Versus Developmental Arrest," by Ozzie Siegel, psychologist, president of the Society, focused on what he called "a major controversy" that has developed "around two major models and theories of psychopathology and treatment: conflict versus deficit." The conflict theory is Freudian, the deficit theory, referring to the unmet needs of the growing child at various stages of psychosexual development, started with Dr. D. W. Winnicott and Dr. W. R. D. Fairbairn, British analysts.

Siegel explained: "The self-psychology theorists, most prominent of whom is Kohut, argue that arrested areas of ego development — the patient's inability to affirm the reality of certain events, the failure to have achieved differentiation, integration and consolidation of self and object representations — necessitate specific technical modifications such as the use of non-interpretative, mirroring interventions in the treatment of such patients. The conflict theorists, on the other hand, continue to call attention to the dangers inherent in ignoring conflict, even in patients with developmental deficits."

Siegel said he had tentatively concluded that Langs' theory of "the concept of adaptive context, derivative communication and an appreciation of the unconscious aspects of the therapeutic interaction, coupled with a better understanding of the distinctive anxieties,

concerns and varieties of psychopathology associated with developmental deficit, along with the understanding that conflict and deficit
coexist, gives us the best opportunity for treating this group of
patients. . . . I am suggesting that an appreciation of the special way
such patients experience loss, separation, disapproval, failure, success, achievement and disappointment enhances our listening, containing, holding and interpretative capacities."

Siegel believes the conflict and deficit theories are not in opposition. Everyone has to solve universal conflicts that occur at certain
psychosexual stages in life. Each of us goes through developmental
phases during which we separate emotionally from our mother and
learn to handle conflicts by the use of defenses. The conflict and
deficit theories are interwoven in our emotions and thoughts.

The *Newsletter* also held a contribution in the *Letters From
Our Readers* column, signed by Marylee Miller, social worker and
secretary of the Society. She looked at Langs' work with perceptive,
humorous eyes. Addressing "My Dear Herr Doktor Freud," she
explains:

"Herr Dokter Langs has discovered that within the therapeutic
setting an interaction takes place which has an effect upon both participants, and yes, he has found that even the person to be healed
at times functions as the healer, albeit in an unconscious manner.
Furthermore, the healer creates a disturbance (for lack of a better
word since it has a perjorative connotation) within the framework
that you set down, with everything he/she says, thus creating an occurrence with which the one to be healed must grapple. Herr Doktor
Langs calls this occurrence the adaptive context. The one to be healed
(or designated patient) responds to the healer (designated analyst)
around this adapative context, many times in a disguised and encoded way (the derivatives). Now then, the patient's unconscious
derivatives can be understood when they organize around this adaptive context which may or may not be clearly/manifestly stated by
the patient.

"Ach, du liebe, my dear Herr Doktor Freud, this creates such
a strain on the analyst, to be aware of his/her counter-transference
as well as what Herr Doktor Langs calls non-countertransference.
You see that, too, exists and can interfere with the analysis of the

patient if the analyst remains oblivious to the manifestations of his/ her own pathology within this dyad. Dear Herr Doktor Freud, you above all can appreciate the enormity of this feat — you have scrutinized yourself in daily self-analysis in order to provide this amazing, nein, brilliant legacy we now cherish."

Faculty, students and staff shared that special enthusiasm and devotion seen in a unified group embarking on new horizons. There was a mutual spirit of earnest inquiry and comradeship as members greeted each other and buoyed up each other with humor. One student said sarcastically, "I'd love to hear material that comes out a *secure* frame," implying every therapist seemed to be a deviator, a dirty word in Langs' lexicon.

Several members of the faculty spoke to me of their experiences with Langs. Martin Greene, professor of social work at Adelphi University, said:

> From Bob, I gained a view of the psychotherapeutic process that was infinitely complex, deeply creative and exquisitely rational. I found him to be a decent, likeable person, caught up in his own ideas but easy to be with, a rather down-to-earth man deeply committed to his work. While his readiness to state unpleasant truths can be disturbing, once you know him, this is softened by his total lack of animosity and by his generosity.
>
> Painfully, I came to the realization that I had previously been working on a purely manifest level, almost totally unaware of the latent messages being communicated by both the patient and myself. Especially upsetting were the patient's unconscious perceptions, at that point mostly negative views of me as often being either confused or erratic, states I was somewhat aware of but had no idea my patients were too. No longer was I able to find refuge in attributing negative perceptions to the patient's primitive pathology.
>
> I now realize that the approach to psychotherapy that I teach and practice is terribly difficult to master. Bob is fond of saying, 'The human mind wasn't made for doing sound psychotherapy'. And he is so very right. Contrary to the popular wisdom that all one needs is the wish to help and a lot of empathy, it takes years of learning and self-scrutiny to master the

communicative approach to psychoanalytic psychotherapy. It takes time to learn to listen to derivative, interactional communications, more time to organize the multitude of words, images, and emotions expressed in any one session, and even more time to formulate a sound, well-timed, and meaningful intervention. The harsh fact is that the patient often needs and may demand more than the therapist can give.

Listening to Bob's analysis of clinical material, sharing in his amazing ability to understand the full and rich tapestry of human interaction, is an exhilarating and ever-inspiring experience. His delineation of specific criteria for organizing and formulating interventions provides invaluable guidelines that serve to make psychotherapy a comprehensible process with specific content to be learned and practiced. At the same time psychotherapy remains a uniquely personal and individual experience, with each therapist bringing his or her unique style of working, to be reflected in the unique experience that is bound to be peculiar to each specific therapeutic pair.

Dr. Joel M. Schwartz, a psychiatrist, who has been supervised by Langs, says there are several reasons Langs' theories "have drawn and held me to them." He explains:

> I have worked in inpatient and outpatient settings, in public as well as private clinics and hospitals. In all of these settings, as well as throughout my psychiatric residency training, reading, and personal therapy, there had always remained too many questions left unanswered to satisfy me. I felt frustrated that it did not seem possible to organize the various theories of our field into a coherent whole.
>
> I had begun to feel like what has been described in our literature as an "as-if" character with regard to the particular technique of therapy I was practicing at any given time. It was as if I were mouthing the words of this therapist or that without any real confidence other than the word of an authority or the subjective opinion of a particular analyst that this was the correct way to proceed.
>
> It was thus with great relief that I came upon the work of Langs who had discovered a level of *listening* and a method of understanding that could allow me to rely upon my patient

to validate my interventions and teach me how to help him. This was a learning-to-learn model which encouraged true growth and autonomy for both the patient and therapist.

It is a difficult task to practice psychotherapy in a manner in which the therapist takes full responsibility for his errors and unresolved conflicts in a way which acknowledges the patient's perceptions of these realities, yet it now seems to be the only way to help patients resolve their neuroses in a lasting and meaningful way. I am greatly concerned about the state of the art of our field, the lack of professional controls of the quality and validity of the therapy which is offered, and the extreme vulnerability and almost total naiveté of the psychotherapy consumer.

Gloria Rich, a psychologist, third-year student, and supervisor, said that a question often heard from beginning therapists is "How can I be supportive to the patient?" Ms. Rich says, "The beginning therapist usually says too much and talks frequently during the patient's session. The supervisor has many aspects to weigh in terms of what and how to teach the comunicative approach. The supervisor can proceed in a more organized way than in other approaches."

First, there is the teaching of the frame issues and how these have an impact upon the patients' material. Encompassed within this is the teaching of the listening process, training the therapist to hear the patients' material as derivative communications, as encoded messages, as unconscious perceptions of the current state of the treatment.

In this approach the therapist becomes painfully aware of the extremely important effect he has on the patient. The frame deviations that are the adaptive contexts around which the patients' material focuses are frequently accompanied by severe acting out, anxiety reactions, and major disruptions in the patients' lives. For the therapist there is no road that leads to safety. In other analytic supervisions, when disruptive aspects in the therapy are examined, the therapist is frequently soothed by discussion of the patient's pathology and questionable genetic hypotheses are promoted. This then becomes a safety zone for both the therapist and the supervisor. Without this safety zone the therapist is again forced to face the full im-

pact he has on the condition of the patient's life. The full realization that one may have such a powerful effect on another
person's life can be frightening. Therefore, the supervisor of
this technique finds his supervisee is more often silent in his
work with patients rather than indulging in the more common
garden variety mistake of abundant questioning and loquaciousness. In addition, in interacting with the supervisor, the
therapist may have a need to narcissistically preserve the image of himself as "the good therapist" which becomes an im-
possibility in the communicative approach.

Langs conducts his share of the teaching, using the cases of
students to illustrate his theories. Since many of the students are fairly new to analytic thinking (some are just starting their personal analyses), occasionally Langs comes across as brusque and critical, using short cuts to a knowledge of which they may be, as yet, unaware.
Initially he may arouse anxiety as a father figure, but as students
come to know him they find him inherently warm and realize he follows criticism with encouragement as he tells them he knows it takes
months to absorb the difficult concepts and their application to the
self. He repeats the concepts in different but applicable words and
in new depths. He seems to care for the beginning therapists, wants
to keep them from starting off on what he believes deviant paths.

He says, "I must take into account the needs of the patient who
is supervised. It is important the therapist know what's going on.
It's far more hurtful to lie or to avoid a supervisory intervention than
to state the truth."

Paula Mosher of Albany, a social worker in her second year
of the three-year program, says, "When I first read Langs, I didn't
understand this new language. It took a year to integrate. Langs'
work has an emotional impact because there is so much emphasis
on you, rather than the patient. You deal with things about yourself you don't necessarily like. It's similar to being in therapy except you are much harsher with yourself than any therapist would
be."

She describes the first year student as looking a bit "peaked,"
adding, "but by the second year you know what you're struggling
with — it's yourself. And by the end of the third year, I imagine you

feel fairly confident about your ability to carry out the communicative approach."

Marc Lubin, Dean of Faculty at the Illinois School of Professional Psychology in Chicago, is head of the Society's Chicago chapter (chapters are forming in other cities, including Denton, Texas, Fort Lauderdale and Montreal). He says:

> As I realized from my own exposure to analytic work over the years, something fundamental was missing in the ways ideas and techniques were being taught and transmitted. Too many assumptions were made about learning these basics. Too many assumptions were also made about automatic competency and validations of interventions. Langs (and Dr. Merton Gill) simultaneously seemed to be challenging the "mystique" of technique with a fresh and thoughtful attention to the subtle processes of the therapeutic interaction.
>
> So I went through the two volumes about technique and then ordered *The Bipersonal Field,* which contained transcripts of Langs' supervisory work. Again, I was intrigued to observe his attention to detail and his respect for the meanings embedded in subtle communications. Only Dr. Bruno Bettelheim had shown a similar genius for extracting powerful implications out of supposedly innocuous exchanges between patient and therapist. I was deeply impressed with Langs' capacity to enliven the patient's commentaries with moment-to-moment significance — in ways that were rich and deeply respectful of the delicateness and primitivity of the analytic relationship — from both sides. He offered the interactional dimension I had always found so useful, and did so in a systematic and yet rich and creative fashion.
>
> From both therapeutic and teaching perspectives I found his work enormously meaningful for myself and my students. I think he has integrated a range of analytic perspectives in a very evocative way. While outsiders might accuse him of being too "rigid," in actuality his approach to clinical material is more extensive, incorporative and comprehensive than any other. In essence, he demonstrates a deeper respect for the range of analytic theory and insight than any other analyst-writer I have read.

To sum up: Langs' capacity to appreciate and respect the interactional field, to offer perspectives for understanding and assessing it, and to provide extensive connections between current psychoanalytic theory and the psychoanalytic situation have revitalized my own teaching and therapeutic work to a great degree.

Lorna Gale Cheifetz, psychologist, from Chicago, said of Langs' work:

I think much of what distinguishes it from the work of others is his emphasis on remaining open to the data rather than trying to fit patients into existing theoretical constructs. The specificity of his technique provides a means of scrutinizing the many factors that potentially influence the therapeutic situation. It details a method of maintaining a secure and stable therapeutic environment. Now, when I find myself reacting to a patient in either a positive or negative fashion, or, if I'm feeling confused, I have a means of analyzing the interaction before taking any action. With Langs' technique, I am able to organize my patients' associations in a way that enables me to understand the rich complexity of each patient as he relates to me. I am able to understand his perceptions of me, both accurate and inaccurate, and am able to glean the origin of these perceptions. The technique provides a method of interpreting the patient's perceptions with his multivariant unconscious meanings in a way that he finds meaningful. It allows me to recognize my errors and my valid interventions. My patients seem to internalize the increased stability and clarity of communication and it is reflected in their outside relationships.

Two members of the Society from out of town who attended this annual meeting told of the deep resentment of their analysts when they made comments on the couch quoting Langs. The analysts became so angry they asked these patients to go elsewhere for treatment. But other classical analysts have been able to successfully work through such material with their patients.

At a general session Langs introduced Searles as "one of the most gifted and innovative clinicians in the history of psychoanalysis." Searles briefly discussed his treatment of schizophrenia, saying, "I sometimes let a patient know a lot about me, some of the more besieged aspects, you might say. The patient does not seem destroyed by my revelations."

He pointed out that therapists face "a lot of depression in work with very ill patients. Many therapists experience such work as extremely anxiety-provoking. Such patients tend to enrage you. You become the major repository of the primitive rage in the room. Some of the rage is even too primitive to put into words, the patient remains mute. His silence is the closest he can get to violence."

In discussing Searles' talk, Dr. James S. Grotstein, of Los Angeles, author of *Splitting and Projective Identification,* commented that the therapist is perceived by the patient to be like his mother, and the mother of a schizophrenic is "a highly selfish, self-involved person who desires her child to serve her — she is in charge, she will not let him go, she keeps him trapped in her world for her own purposes. To grow normally, a child needs a mother who will guarantee boundaries and release him. The child of the mother who has trapped him in her world feels if he grows up he is taking his body away from his mother and she needs it. So all he has left is regression to the depressive position of infancy."

The schizophrenic is telling the therapist, Grotstein said, " 'I've been threatened with oblivion, cast into oblivion,' and anyone in the presence of so tormented a person feels how he wants to cease to exist."

Langs spoke on "Madness in Psychotherapy," the title of a book on which he is working. It is based on his interviews with twenty patients (not his own) treated by therapists ranging from classical analysts to those practicing EST, Gestalt and other therapies. All the patients were college graduates, eleven were therapists themselves. Of a total of seventy-three therapists consulted by the twenty patients, fifty-two did some form of active therapy, as contrasted to psychoanalysis.

Langs reported: "After I conducted each three-hour interview, I was drained. 'Utter madness,' I thought. Madness is the coin of the realm, the medium of communication. Not one of these patients had a secure frame. Not a single comment by a therapist sounded like a valid interpretation. Those who tried to interpret used clichés. Some said to the patient, 'You can interpret better than I can'."

In addition to such physical contact as kissing and embracing, there was sexual intimacy between a number of patients and therapists. One patient, a virgin, was seduced by her first therapist. When she finally got the courage to leave, she suffered a psychotic break. Another patient, when her therapist tried to rape her, had persistent fantasies of murdering him. One patient told Langs that a therapist tried to teach her to use a vibrator, saying he used it with the women he slept with.

Langs called such deviations "acts of madness and defenses against madness" by therapists. Both patient and therapist share the madness, he added, in that every patient he interviewed had remained in treatment with such a therapist for quite a while. This blindness occurs, he believes, because a patient looks up to the therapist, thinks he has found the perfect therapist and has to defend this fantasy even when it is strongly contradicted by the behavior of the therapist.

The feelings of those studying with Langs seemed to be summed up at the annual meeting by Natalie Becker, a psychologist and member of the Society. She said, "I found his supervision extremely valuable in developing a technique for listening and understanding the unconscious process and interaction between patient and therapist."

There were wistful looks as the participants bid each other goodbye and prepared to leave for their homes — Sweden, for the one psychologist, and all over the United States for the rest. I thanked Langs and Audrey McGhie, administrative director of the psychotherapy program.

The words of a departing psychiatrist from Texas remained with me: "I felt deep anguish at how my patients over the years before I met Langs had suffered because I hadn't really heard what they were telling me about how I was breaking the ground rules."

Then he added, with a sigh, "My unconscious had known all along it was wrong."

12
BEYOND LANGS

A sign of the growing acceptance of Langs' theories has been their application not only to psychotherapeutic process but also to other areas. They have been written about in regard to the mother-child relationship, the *object relations* theory, the treatment of disturbed children and the world of the theater. These applications are described in *Listening and Interpretation in Therapy,* edited by Dr. James Raney.

In this book Dr. Merton Gill says Langs "has produced a rich, voluminous, complex, tightly organized, albeit often repetitive, system prescribing and defining the technique of psychoanalysis and psychoanalytic psychotherapy." Gill adds that "in large part" he agrees with Langs' main ideas but also has some "serious disagreements."

He explains: "I believe the disagreements are a reflection of the extent to which Langs remains a captive of classical — and I mean prevalent, not Freud's — psychoanalysis." Gill thinks the prevailing practice labeled "classical" has "departed significantly from Freud's practice, which would, more appropriately, be called 'classical'."

Gill lists seven points of agreement with Langs. The first he describes as "a shift in attitude towards a greater egalitarianism [equality] in assessing patient and analyst. The analyst is a participant and he always, to a greater or less degree, participates pathologically. . . . The analyst is a participant observer and we are all much more simply human than otherwise."

The second: "Not only is the analytic situation a bipersonal field with appropriate and inappropriate inputs from both participants but inappropriate inputs, in varying proportions with appropriate inputs, are ubiquitously present. One must therefore say that transference and countertransference are continuous rather than occasional, the latter being the classical position."

The third: "These transferences and countertransferences are primarily expressed in disguised and allusive form in the patient's associations and the analyst's interventions. These disguised associations and interventions are derivatives of the transference and countertransferences to which they allude." He adds that transferences and countertransferences are regarded as "occasional in the classical view." This "results in the failure of the classical analyst to give adequate attention to the fact that the [patient's] associations and [analyst's] interventions are derivatives of such transferences and countertransferences."

The fourth: "Not only because the field is a bipersonal one but also because of the purpose for which it has been established, it is around the relationship between analyst and patient that the associations and interventions are in fact primarily organized. It is this relationship therefore which should be the focus of the analyst's interpretations. . . . The analysis of the transference in the here and now should be the primary focus of work in the therapy. In contrast, the classical view in practice, if not in theory, places at least equal emphasis on extratransference interpretation, both contemporary and genetic [applying to the past], whether intrapsychic or interactional."

The fifth: "The analyst's interventions are hypotheses whose correctness or incorrectness can be determined only in terms of the patient's ensuing associations." While at first this might seem a tenet of classical analysis, the difference in Langs' view, Gill says, "is that, once again, he belittles the relevance to validation of an intervention of conscious associations bearing on that intervention and emphasizes almost exclusively validation by encoded derivatives [the unconscious meaning], as already defined." Gill believes that while derivatives deserve more attention, conscious associations are important too.

The sixth: "Desirable change in the patient results not only from insight but from the experience of a good relationship with the therapist. The classical point of view, with some notable and increasing exceptions, places much less emphasis on the experience of the relationship as a mutative factor, indeed often to the extent of considering change in which the experience plays any significant role as an evidence of unresolved transference and therefore that the process has been 'psychotherapeutic' rather than 'psychoanalytic'." He adds that evidence of the beneficent experience "is again primarily to be found, at least at first, in associations which are derivatives, that is, which in their manifest content refer to a good experience with someone other than the therapist."

The seventh: In most instances the essentials of the therapeutic process should be the same — psychoanalytic — whatever the nature of the disorder and the frequency of sessions, whether the patient sits in a chair or lies on the couch and whatever the experience of the therapist. This differs from the classical view which specifies only certain people are analyzable, a frequency of at least four times a week, lying on the couch, and the therapist trained in psychoanalysis. The position taken by Langs, with which Gill says he agrees, is often mistaken, he says, as equivalent to saying there is no difference between psychotherapy and psychoanalysis.

"Far from saying that, it says that the range of applicability of psychoanalysis is far wider than is generally considered to be the case," Gill explains. "I believe the term psychotherapy should be reserved for the application of the principles described above in only truncated, partial ways. It is my view of the wide applicability of analytic technique which results in my using the terms analyst and therapist and analysis and therapy interchangeably in this chapter."

Gill comments on the difference between Langs and himself when it comes to the ground rules. He maintains Langs "is correct in saying that the frame plays an important role in the patient's experience of the relationship. It is also true that the way the analyst manages the frame is of vital importance. But he assumes that for some features, such as absolute confidentiality, there is only one correct frame and that for other features deviations from the frame, once set, are universally and inevitably experienced by the patient as harmful. . . . Langs insists that flexibility about changing a patient's hour cannot truly be experienced by a patient as a friendly accommodation rather than, for example, an inability to bear the patient's reaction to a refusal and thus a betrayal of the analyst's ability to 'hold' the patient. Langs assumes all patients want to be 'held' in the same way. To argue for flexibility is not necessarily to overlook that a change in the frame may have an important significance to the patient, a significance which may well be disguised. But a refusal ever to change the frame may be experienced as uncompromising rigidity. I believe that Langs' overall attitude may be experienced this way by some, if not many, of his patients."

Gill says he believes it is possible to have audio recordings for research in the therapeutic process "without damage" to the patient if the therapeutic situation is "an otherwise good one." He disagrees with Langs' statement that silence is one of the three appropriate interventions, the other two being maintenance of the ground rules and interpretations. Gill sides with Dr. Samuel Lipton's belief that "silence should mean only that the analyst is *listening*, not that he is employing it as an *intervention*."

I thought how much artistry, understanding and sense of timing must go into each interpretation so the patient will use it, not reject it angrily or refuse to hear it. For some interpretations (I later realized) I had waited months, perhaps years, until the analyst decided the time was right, and that I might finally accept them. For instance, if he had told me earlier there was still much of the dependent child in me, the interpretation would have brought forth fury. Only when I had been allowed the time to realize how infantile I was in certain respects, could he say about a specific situation, "You still wish to be a child," and I knew he was right, that much of my past unhappy behavior had stemmed from an inability to achieve enough emotional freedom from my mother and father. Not many of us realize the strength of those early bonds if parents have not helped us to break free.

Gill also thinks that questions, confrontations and clarification by the analyst, as well as interpretations, can play an important role in revealing the patient's conscious thoughts and "in formulating what has not yet been given verbal shape." He criticizes Langs' presentation of his theories "in a way which is seriously interfering with the recognition and acceptance of the sense in which they are valid," referring to Langs' dogmatism. Gill calls this "most unfortunate."

In another chapter of the book, Gill's critique is countered by Marc Lubin, Dean of Faculty, Illinois School of Professional Psychology, who has studied with both Gill and Langs. In his chapter, "Views on Neurosis, Listening, and Cure," Lubin discusses the two areas in which, he says, Gill defines his major disagreements with Langs: the nature of the interpersonal reality within the therapeutic relationship, and the significance of the patient's conscious experience of the relationship.

Gill's problem with Langs' view on transference, the frame, therapeutic technique and validation "derives from their basic disagreement about the primacy of unconscious forces in neurosis, and the significance of listening to and encouraging derivative communication of these unconscious forces as the key to the resolution of neurosis," Lubin says.

Gill also does not organize his analysis of derivatives around the specific types of adaptive contexts, as Langs does, and these differences in approach, "as well as some misunderstanding of Langs' position, lead Gill to significantly distort Langs' contributions by confusing him with the 'classical' analyst."

Gill's differences with Langs "are most dramatic" in the area of interventions and "flow most clearly from the distinctions between their approaches to neurosis, listening and cure." To Gill, preconscious and inhibited conscious expressions are critical elements in uncovering and working through the patient's disturbances. In contrast, Langs believes "conscious and direct thoughts about the therapist reflect only a small and minimally conflictual portion of the patient's neurosis; Langs does not believe active pursuit of even consciously withheld ideas reveals any significant information about the core of the patient's pathology." The pursuit of consciously withheld material, to Langs, only results in brief emotional discharge for the patient and extended intellectualization and rumination.

"It isn't that manifest transference material is 'suspect'," Lubin says. "It simply can do no more than carry meanings the patient *already* knows. Encoded image and narrative derivatives carry meanings the patient seeks to hide from himself and from the therapist, meanings so disturbing they must be encoded to escape detection. Fleeting conscious thoughts about the therapist are indicators of a disturbance but in themselves rarely yield significant information about the patient's more disturbing perceptions of and reactions to the therapist."

The application of Langs' theories to the psychoanalytic process are discussed by Masud Khan, a Persian prince who became a psychoanalyst in Great Britain, in the chapter, "Negotiating the Impossible." Khan explains he has undertaken to examine the implications of Freud's use of the verbs "negotiate" and "relate to," and the adjective "impossible," contained in Freud's statement in 1925 that "there are three impossible professions — educating, healing, governing."

He asserts: "Freud's 'method' calls for an as-if 'programmed intimacy' and a *contest*. The analyst has *some* knowledge, or so he believes, and is rigorously *educated* to believe, of what this 'programmed intimacy' would entail. The understanding of the patient's contribution, masked by his symptoms, if he has the facility to 'speak' thus, will constitute most of the inter-action of relating between him and his analyst, and their discourse. By using the verb 'negotiating', I want to indicate and emphasize the highly precarious and tentative character of the *commitment* that the analyst offers/imposes, and to which the patient becomes an unknowing *accomplice* to his, the patient's complicity. This double bind, or paradox, is the very essence of the *relating*, which must not grow into a 'relationship', because that would make it an *enacted* intimacy, and which must not lose impetus through the *lacking* relationship, otherwise the game is over.

"Hence my use of the adjective 'impossible'. Both the analyst and the patient bring to this relating in the analytic situation their individuated styles of 'self-cure'. Only the analyst's 'self-cure' is sanctified for him by personal belief and professional accrediting, and the patient's is in question, both by the patient and his analyst. As the dialogues between Langs and Searles and Langs and Stone demonstrate eloquently, and, thank God, with humour and goodwill on each side, this distribution of roles in the 'programmed intimacy' and contest, undergo devastating vicissitudes, not only of 'material' (as it is called) but of the roles themselves."

Khan pays tribute to Langs, describing him as "prolific and erudite a reader as he is a copious writer." Khan says that in the area of clinical formulations, "Langs' fervor for debating and questioning strikes me as both refreshing and purposeful in a creative, sharing way."

Khan points out that Freud "did not invent the analytic setting and method in one fell swoop of inspiration and insight. It took him years to arrive at a basic clinical frame and the necessary tools (concepts) with which to function in it."

In spite of, or perhaps because of, the mammoth literature about and around Freud's "method," one simple fact has never been singled out for discussion — Freud's "extraordinary *demands* on the patient," Khan says. In no society, primitive or industrialized, did "a shaman or a physician, until Freud, ever demand of a patient to come for a limited time of sixty minutes a day, six times a week, for an unpredictable length of time. . . . It may seem banal and rather fatuous to emphasize this, but its implications, if we pause to consider them, are monumental and revolutionary indeed."

What makes the discussion of changes in Freud's therapeutic aims and ambitions difficult, Khan says, "is the fact that he himself never spelt out the theme with any consistency. His papers on technique are more in the nature of cautionary admonitions than precepts to be rigorously obeyed. One can, all the same, chart out the changing aims of psychotherapy from 'transforming hysterical misery into common unhappiness' [1895] to 'the aim of the treatment will never be anything but the *practical* recovery of the patient, the restoration of his ability to lead an active life and his capacity for enjoyment [1904].' Freud's 'method' at this stage he states as: 'an art of interpretation.'"

Khan asserts that Freud's "method," described by him in such words as "conquering" and "mastery," seeks "a commitment that involves both parties, unequally." This commitment entails "a two-way demand. A *demand* on the *patient* and a *demand* by the patient." He adds, "Freud's 'method' *instructs* both demands."

The "demand on the patient," Khan says, is regulated through analysis of the patient. He describes this as "an apprenticeship that inevitably teaches in learning *the how* if not the what (which still remains vague and allusive, if not illusive), of making the demand."

The "demand from the patient" is initiated by proffering him a setting and a possibility of "intimacy," the character and function of which the person, as a patient, at the beginning "has not many clues to; but which will soon engulf him and his analyst in utterly unpredicated amplitudes of relating and refusing to relate (each in his own style)." The difference is that the style of the analyst is considered "normal" and that of the patient as conditioned by his childhood experiences and unconscious fantasies, both sexual and aggressive. Gradually, the as-if "mutual" undertaking, labeled the "therapeutic alliance," takes on, Khan says, "the climate and character of a contest! When this contest is benign, it allows for playing, healing and recovery; and when it goes sour, it is damaging to both participants, and there is no remedy to that!" He adds it is from choice that he writes in a colloquial manner "because all these issues have been linguistically petrified by our metapsychology: especially in its clinical formulations."

In another chapter, "The Higher Implications of Langs' Contributions," Dr. James S. Grotstein, of the Los Angeles Psychoanalytic Institute, calls Langs' article, "Modes of 'Cure' in Psychoanalysis and Psychoanalytic Psychotherapy," published in 1981 in the *International Journal of Psycho-Analysis*, "a veritable challenge to all psychoanalysts and all psychotherapy."

Langs' "rhetoric, although certainly not rude or contumacious, urgently challenges all practitioners to re-examine the very meaning of the therapy they do, of the transferences they interpret, of the very interpretations they call interpretations, of their interventions and silences, of every aspect of their procedures," Grotstein says.

He maintains that Langs is addressing one of the most crucial elements in psychoanalysis: "How do we cure a patient? How do we make optimal benefit of the transference? Put another way, how do we metapsychologize the interaction between the patient and the therapist and utilize the very point Greenson was one of the first to discover, the real relationship to the patient? . . . Somehow most traditional analysts believe that a mere reference to transference feelings is enough to allow a therapeutic discharge to take place, and that is all that needs to be done."

Grotstein describes psychoanalysis as "a special form of observation in which the subject of observation and the object of observation are both altered by that act of observation. . . . The analyst's

observation of his patient changes the patient. The patient's observation of himself changes the patient." The patient's observation of
the analyst is another important factor in the patient's change and
can be either "a beneficent change or a malevolent stagnation."

The analyst's capacity "to abandon memory and desire" so as
to achieve detached observation "is one of the gifts we offer the patient which at the same time is his entitlement of us — all to the effect of establishing an analytic space, a transitional space between
the therapist and the patient where the analytic scenario can take
place — more like a holy passion play, a sacred drama, or even a
joyous play than not, but, whatever else, always Revelation."

This space "bespeaks a hallowed and revered area between the
patient and the therapist much like the space between the infant and
its mother where nursing takes place. The empathic, vicarious, participant-observer metaphor, however, conveys a bonding, a postnatal
continuation of umbilical at-one-ment, if you will," Grotstein said.
"The Taoists put it poetically: 'A finger flickers and a star quivers'!"

The two ways of listening to a patient, "and listening to oneself
while listening to a patient," suggest specific application of a dual-
track theory of human existence, Grotstein says. Freud explored this
concept but "unfortunately ignored it when he depersonalized and
disenfranchised the unconscious as an inferior function, when he
made it an 'object' of inquiry rather than allowing it to be the ego's
partner and 'co-subject'."

Grotstein mentions the analyst's function in helping the patient
understand the repetition compulsion in the transference (where the
patient unconsciously repeats the past in relation to the therapist).
He comments, "At depth we [the patients] are best able to complete
an experience and therefore to mourn it, say good-bye to it, and for-
get it, when we know that there is an object present who is as *attuned* to us in such an empathic bond of rapport and yet at the same
time separate from us and sufficiently unvictimized so as to convince us that he has survived his own experiences and can pull us
into our future safely — and we can then be through with the experience."

The communicative approach recognizes that the patient functions unconsciously to the therapist as a persistent supervisor who

is not easily evaded, according to Dr. James Raney, editor of the book and a psychiatrist in Seattle, in his chapter, "Narcissistic Defensiveness and the Communicative Approach."

Raney maintains that another "not inconsiderable barrier [to the acceptance of Langs] may be the differences between aspects of the communicative approach and the methods of the therapist's own analyst: It is very difficult to break an unconsciously acquired tradition, based upon idealizaton and identification with one's own analyst. This is especially true where the idealization and identification has been defensively determined, based upon what is now known to be erroneous interventions and faulty technique."

He suggests that perhaps the larger group of psychoanalytic practitioners and creative thinkers "needs more time to digest and evaluate the concepts of Langs. . . . Every new advance is based on hard work and meets opposition. Contributions to the advancement of psychotherapy and psychoanalysis that are inherent in most of the criticisms shall remain unrealized until the critics can adopt a more scientific and less personal approach."

He believes the absence of more objective discussion and citation of Langs' work is a "manifestation of the defensiveness stimulated by the inherent potential for self-exposure and narcissistic disturbance of the approach." He adds, "The 'silence' of creative writers in the literature appears to be a result of defensiveness stemming from the disturbance of this narcissism from the self-observing and revealing potential of Langs' theories."

In addition, Langs' ideas constitute "a new paradigm that threatens the narcissistic investment in other theoretical approaches practiced by most therapists," Raney concludes. He suggests that a "reworking by these writers of some of their own cases in the light of the communicative approach would considerably advance the science and practice of psychotherapy."

Another contributor to the book, Maury Neuhaus, psychologist, associate director of the Lenox Hill Hospital Psychotherapy Program, discusses how the communicative approach has implemented clinically the essence of Dr. W. R. D. Fairbairn's theory of "object relations."

Fairbairn believes that the significance of living lies in object relationships, "that only through relationships can our life have meaning, for without object relations the ego cannot develop." Neuhaus explains, "The real loss of all objects would be tantamount to psychic death. A repressed inner world of internalized bad objects is the result of bad external relations in infancy. The inner psychic world duplicates the original, frustrating one." The patient can only relinquish attachment to "bad" objects safely when these internal "bad" objects are replaced by the positive introjective aspects of the therapist.

Neuhaus is also director of the West Side Psychological and Educational Center in New York City, whose staff has been trained in psychotherapy at the Lenox Hill program. The Center provides diagnostic services to children from three years of age through college. It also offers professional training in supervision of analytic psychotherapy and diagnostic testing, using Langs' theories.

Another application of Langs' work is to the mother-child relationship. Joan B. Erdheim, instructor and supervisor at the Training Institute for Mental Health Practitioners in New York, in "The Development of Communicative Modes in the Mother-Child Relationship," suggests that the "separation-individuation" process described by Dr. Margaret Mahler not only enables the emergence "of the intrapsychic self-object world" but is responsible for the full development of an interpersonal communicative style similar to what Langs calls Type A (his communicative approach) or Type B and C (therapeutic approaches built on understanding only conscious communication).

The mother's communicative style and her use of it is crucial in determining the baby's communicative style, Erdheim maintains. The mother who can allow her child slowly to achieve emotional independence uses her feelings "not for riddance or battle needs but to more intimately understand what her youngster is experiencing and to better know how to intervene." Such a mother may even "give a gentle push out of the nest."

Langs' work as it applies to the theater is discussed by Vera M. Jiji, professor of psychology, literature and drama at Brooklyn

College, in the chapter "Pinter's Use of Language and Character Interaction Compared to Langs' Theories of Communication." She points out that Harold Pinter's "realistic dialogues use effectively the kind of language uttered by patients on the couch. It is a language that contains hidden messages. Speech in Pinter serves as a vehicle for carrying the underlying meaning. Pinter's work is unique in that his characters' *primary* source of power lies in their ability to use language to control or mystify others, resembling Langs' Type B and C patients."

Dr. Roy Mendlesohn, director of the Growth Center in St. Louis, a nonprofit outpatient clinic for troubled children, writes how Langs' work has influenced the treatment of emotionally disturbed children. He reports that autistic children, divorced from the world of reality, shutting out all human relationships, taught him "in some difficult and painful ways" that he, as therapist, had been offering them many different forms "of a pathological relationship."

He says, "I had to look at the fact that each time I offered the children some form of a pathological relationship, they closed me out. At such moments, no relationship was possible. As soon as I showed any willingness and capacity to examine the part I was playing in their experience, they would begin to communicate to me."

He called this "quite a startling experience," one that had a deep and profound impact. It confronted him with the task of constantly exploring his own motivations whenever the children ceased to communicate with him. "Each time I did so," he said, "I was immensely rewarded with human communication from children who otherwise could not communicate at all."

Before this, he had explained the differences he saw in the children and his other patients as those between individuals who were considered analyzable and those who possessed what were described as "ego deficits or developmental arrests." But now, he said, he began to realize he was somehow splitting his experience with these supposedly different groups of patients and became more aware of the powerful influence any pathological or defense interactions on his part had on the psychotherapeutic process with all of his patients. With the children, the effect was immediate, concrete and impossible to deny. With the adults it was more subtle, elusive and easy to deny or rationalize away, usually, he said, with well-formulated psychodynamic explanations.

In describing Langs' visit to the Center, Mendelsohn says: "It is difficult to capture in the written word, the powerful impact these sessions provided for all of us. We immediately discovered we were deeply influenced in our selection of material to present by our unconscious recognition that the love of and search for truth is a process that has to be constantly fought for against extremely strong resistances. We had unconsciously selected therapeutic interactions that offered Dr. Langs an opportunity to teach us how to listen to and respond to the direct and especially encoded messages we were receiving from our patients. He brought this message to us consistently. It was not that the frame or ground rules were to be managed rigidly or inflexibly but rather he brought a clear vision as to how to listen so our patients could tell us what they needed and how to provide it."

The staff learned during this visit and since, he said, that the "difficult task of listening to the truth in our patients depends first on our ability to listen to the truth of ourselves. That task is fraught with dangers. Our natural orientation as human beings is so invested with the need to defend that in order to maintain such a listening posture we need, in addition to the ongoing process of self-analysis, the help of our patients and their unconscious perceptions."

Mendelsohn concluded, "Dr. Langs demands a great deal of a therapist and so he should. He also brings to his work and to his his teaching a great deal of himself. In giving this, he enabled us to see the forceful impact of the powerful lessons our patients had to teach us. He illuminated, amplified and taught us how to listen and learn from the very patients we had been listening to and thought we were learning from for a long time. We knew what he meant when he said, 'Once you see the truth, you have no choice. There is no other direction in which you can move'."

I was left with many images of Langs after reading his books, interviewing him and talking to psychoanalysts, psychiatrists, psychologists and social workers who have heard him explain his theories or studied with him. Some, like Dr. Mendlesohn, could not praise him enough. Others called him opinionated, dogmatic, rigid, contentious, overzealous and impatient, criticized him for never using his own cases.

Some were uncomfortable with his personal manner — he can be rather like a runaway train as he races through supervision of a case, peremptorily dismissing all argument. He feels his peers should be able to understand what he is saying, even though intellectually he knows resistances are high because his theories are critical of therapists who break ground rules, who do not "listen" to patients voicing hurt and anger and who make useless and senseless interpretations or fail to make helpful ones.

He says philosophically, "I have worked hard in my professional career for what I believe in and while I wish I were more accepted by the classical psychoanalysts under whom I trained, I am grateful for those who do accept my work and for the growing number of psychiatrists, psychologists and social workers who believe in my theories. This means patients will be getting more effective therapy — which has been my goal."

Psychoanalysis is in the process of evolving, as with any science. Freud set the blueprint but contemporary analysts have made important discoveries in child development, the treatment of the very emotionally disturbed, the role of hostility and the training of psychoanalysts. Of the last, as Dr. Jacob Arlow says in the Memorial Issue (1982, Volume II) for Dr. Joan Fleming of the *Annual of Psychoanalysis*, published by the Chicago Institute for Psychoanalysis, there is still much to be understood about the training of psychoanalysts.

As with all discoveries, time alone will verify the validity of Langs' work. Perhaps his findings will have an impact on the training of psychotherapists so that more effective ones will be available to those who seek help. Perhaps even the classical psychoanalysts, if they have been breaking ground rules, will hew more closely to them. We can also hope that greater numbers of the general public will examine more carefully the qualifications of the therapist they select to ease their mental pain.

In essence, this book, and all therapy, is about getting to know the self—an age-old search of Man's ever since Sophocles counseled, "Know thyself." But there are depths beyond depths to the self. The exploration continues, hopefully for a lifetime, after the formal analysis ends and the person listens to the truth of his inner voice in a new way: one he has learned from the analyst.

————

Sometimes one does a book for the fun of it.
Or to learn.
Or for love.
Or revenge.
Or the wish to help others.
Or money.
Or to compete.
Or for reasons unknown.
And sometimes for several or all of these reasons.

————

REFERENCES

Baranger, M., and Baranger, W. (1966). Insight in the analytic situation. In *Psychoanalysis in the Americas,* ed. R. E. Litman, pp. 56–72. New York: International Universities Press.

Blanck, G., and Blanck, R. (1974). *Ego Psychology: Theory and Practice.* New York: Columbia University Press.

———. (1982). Letter to the editor. *International Journal of Psycho-Analysis* 63:87.

Bleger, J. (1967). Psycho-analysis of the psychoanalytic frame. *International Journal of Psycho-Analysis* 48:511–519.

Breuer, J., and Freud, S. (1893–1895). Studies on hysteria. *Standard Edition* 2.

Calef, V. (1979). Review of *The Bipersonal Field,* by R. Langs. *Journal of the American Psychoanalytic Association* 27:702–705.

Casement, P. (1980). Review of *The Therapeutic Environment,* by R. Langs. *International Review of Psycho-Analysis* 7:525–528.

Erdheim, J. B. (1983). The development of communicative modes in the mother-child relationship. In *Listening and Interpretation in Therapy,* ed. J. Raney. New York: Aronson.

Fintzy, R. T. (1978). Review of *The Listening Process,* by R. Langs. *Southern California Psychiatric Society News* 25: p. 9.

———. (1979). Review of *The Therapeutic Interaction: A Synthesis,* by R. Langs. *Southern California Psychiatric Society News* 26:10.

Freeman, L., and Strean, H. S. (1981). *Freud and Women.* New York: Ungar.

Freud, S. (1905). Fragment of an analysis of a case of hysteria. *Standard Edition* 7:1–122.

———. (1910). The future prospects of psycho-analytic therapy. *Standard Edition* 11:139–151.

_____. (1912). Recommendations to physicians practising psycho-analysis. *Standard Edition* 12:109–120.

_____. (1913). On beginning the treatment (further recommendations on the technique of psycho-analysis, I). *Standard Edition* 12:121–144.

_____. (1915). Observations on transference-love (further recommendations on the technique of psycho-analysis, II). *Standard Edition* 12:157–171.

_____. (1916–1917). Introductory lectures on psycho-analysis. *Standard Edition* 15 and 16.

_____. (1919). Lines of advance in psycho-analytic therapy. *Standard Edition* 17:157–168.

Gill, M. (1979). The analysis of the transference. *Journal of the American Psychoanalytic Association* 27(Supplement):263–288.

_____. (1981). Review of *The Therapeutic Environment,* by R. Langs. *Contemporary Psychology* 26:36–37.

_____. (1983). Robert Langs on technique: a critique. In *Listening and Interpretation in Therapy,* ed. J. Raney. New York: Aronson.

Gray, P. (1982). Developmental lag in technique. *Journal of the American Psychoanalytic Association* 30:621–655.

Greenson, R., and Wexler, M. (1969). The non-transference relationship in the psychoanalytic situation. *International Journal of Psycho-Analysis* 50:27–39.

Grotstein, J. (1981). *Splitting and Projective Identification.* New York: Aronson.

_____. (1983). The higher implications of Langs' contributions. In *Listening and Interpretation in Therapy,* ed. J. Raney. New York: Aronson.

Heimann, P. (1949). On countertransference. Paper presented at the 16th International Psycho-Analytic Congress in Zurich. (Printed in *International Journal of Psycho-Analysis* 31:81–84.)

Jackel, M. M. (1978). Review of *The Bipersonal Field,* by R. Langs. *International Journal of Psycho-Analysis* 59:537–539.

Jiji, V. (1983). Pinter's use of language and character interaction compared to the Langs' theories of communication. In *Listen-*

ing and Interpretation in Therapy, ed. J. Raney. New York: Aronson.

Khan, M. (1983). Negotiating the impossible. In *Listening and Interpretation in Therapy,* ed. J. Raney. New York: Aronson.

Klein, M. (1952). The origins of transference. *International Journal of Psycho-Analysis* 33:433-438.

Langs, R. (1971). Day residues, recall residues, and dreams: reality and the psyche. *Journal of the American Psychoanalytic Association* 19:499-523.

———. (1975). The patient's unconscious perceptions of the therapist's errors. In *Tactics and Techniques in Psychoanalytic Therapy,* Volume 2: Countertransference, ed. P. L. Giovacchini, pp. 239-250. New York: Aronson.

———. (1976). *The Bipersonal Field.* New York: Aronson.

———. (1976). *The Therapeutic Interaction,* Volumes I and II. New York: Aronson.

———. (1978). *The Listening Process.* New York: Aronson.

———. (1981). Letter to the editor. *International Journal of Psycho-Analysis* 63:259-260.

———. (1981). Modes of "cure" in psychoanalysis and psychoanalytic psychotherapy. *International Journal of Psycho-Analysis* 62:199-214.

———. (1982). "Feel good" psychotherapy on trial: testimony in Hinckley case shows danger in the technique. *Los Angeles Times,* May 26, 1982.

———. (1982). *Psychotherapeutic Conspiracy.* New York: Aronson.

Langs, R., ed. (1981). *Classics in Psychoanalytic Technique.* New York: Aronson.

Langs, R., and Searles, H. (1980). *Intrapsychic and Interpersonal Dimensions of Treatment.* New York: Aronson.

Langs, R., and Stone, L. (1980). *The Therapeutic Experience and Its Setting.* New York: Aronson.

Little, M. (1951). Countertransference and the patient's response to it. *International Journal of Psycho-Analysis* 32:32-40.

Lubin, M. (1983). Views on neurosis, listening, and cure: a discussion of Gill's comments on Langs. In *Listening and Interpretation in Therapy,* ed. J. Raney. New York: Aronson.

Meissner, W. W. (1978). Review of *The Technique of Psychoanalytic Psychotherapy,* Volumes 1 and 2, by R. Langs. *International Journal of Psycho-Analysis* 59:535–537.

Neuhaus, M. (1983). Communicative psychotherapy and object relations theory. In *Listening and Interpretation in Therapy,* ed. J. Raney. New York: Aronson.

Osman, M. P. (1981). Review of *The Listening Process,* by R. Langs. *Journal of the American Academy of Psychoanalysis* 9:319–323.

Racker, H. (1957). The meanings and uses of countertransference. *Psychoanalytic Quarterly* 26:303–357, 1972.

———. (1968). *Transference and Countertransference.* New York: International Universities Press.

Raney, J. (1983). Narcissistic defensiveness and the communicative approach. In *Listening and Interpretation in Therapy,* ed. J. Raney. New York: Aronson.

Raney, J., ed. (1983). *Listening and Interpretation in Therapy.* New York: Aronson.

Searles, H. (1948). Concerning transference and countertransference. *International Journal of Psychoanalytic Psychotherapy* 7:165–188.

———. (1975). The patient as therapist to his analyst. In *Tactics and Techniques in Psychoanalytic Therapy,* Volume 2: Countertransference, ed. P. L. Giovacchini, pp. 95–151. New York: Aronson.

Siegel, O. (1982). Conflict theory versus development arrest. *Society for Psychoanalytic Psychotherapy Newsletter* Vol. 1, no. 2.

Solomon, R. (1974). Review of *The Technique of Psychoanalytic Psychotherapy,* Volume 1, by R. Langs. *American Journal of Psychiatry* 131:1054.

Stewart, W. A. (1967). *Psychoanalysis: The First Ten Years.* New York: Macmillan.

Stewart, W. A., and Freeman, L. (1972). *The Secret of Dreams.* New York: Macmillan.

Strachey, J. (1934). The nature of the therapuetic action of psycho-analysis. *International Journal of Psycho-analysis* 15:127–159.

Winnicott, D. W. (1960). The theory of the parent-infant relationship. *International Journal of Psycho-Analysis* 41:585–595.

_____. (1971). *Playing and Reality*. New York: Basic Books.

Selected Works of Robert Langs, M.D.